AN ILLUSTRATED A–Z DIRECTORY OF
MILITARY HELICOPTERS

AN ILLUSTRATED A–Z DIRECTORY OF
MILITARY HELICOPTERS

FEATURING OVER 80 HELICOPTERS SHOWN IN MORE THAN
300 HISTORICAL AND MODERN PHOTOGRAPHS

FRANCIS CROSBY

southwater

This edition is published by Southwater,
an imprint of Anness Publishing Ltd,
108 Great Russell Street,
London WC1B 3NA;
info@anness.com

www.southwaterbooks.com; www.annesspublishing.com; twitter: @Anness_Books

Anness Publishing has a new picture agency outlet for images for publishing, promotions or advertising.
Please visit our website www.practicalpictures.com for more information.

© Anness Publishing Ltd 2015

Publisher: Joanna Lorenz
Senior Editor: Felicity Forster
Designer: Nigel Pell
Production Controller: Rosanna Anness

Previously published as part of a larger volume, *The World Encyclopedia of Military Helicopters*

PUBLISHER'S NOTE
Although the information in this book is believed to be accurate and true at the time of going to press, neither the authors nor the publisher can accept any legal responsibility or liability for any errors or omissions that may have been made. The nationality of each helicopter is identified in the relevant specification box by the national flag that was in use at the time of service.

ACKNOWLEDGEMENTS
Picture research for this book was carried out by Jasper Spencer-Smith, who has selected images from JSS Collection and the following (key: l=left, r=right, t=top, b=bottom, m=middle): UK MoD Crown Copyright 2010: 2; 3; 14, 15t, 15b; 18t, 18b; 19; 20b; 23; 27t; 28; 47t; 52t; 58t, 58b; 59t, 59b; 68b; 150t; 152t; 154t, 154b; 155. Every effort has been made to acknowledge photographs correctly, however we apologize for any unintentional omissions, which will be corrected in future editions.

PAGE 1: **Westland Lynx.**
PAGE 2: **Aérospatiale SA 341 Gazelles.**
PAGE 3: **Sikorsky SH-60F Seahawk.**
BELOW LEFT: **AgustaWestland AW101 Merlin.**
BELOW RIGHT: **Hughes OH-6A Cayuse.**
OPPOSITE LEFT: **MBB/Eurocopter Bo105.**
OPPOSITE RIGHT: **Sikorsky HH-60G Pave Hawks.**

Contents

ABOVE: **The Curtiss Bleecker helicopter standing in front of a hangar at the National Advisory Committee for Aeronautics (NACA) in Langley, Virginia, in 1926. The machine was one of many early experimental helicopters that lacked stability and suffered from extreme vibration.**

Introduction

Although the word "helicopter" is derived from the ancient Greek *heli* (twisted, curved) and *pteron* (wing), the word we recognize today was not suggested until the 1860s in France, as *hélicoptère*. Both cultures are, however, pre-dated by the idea of flying in a way that we now associate with helicopters and a few fixed-wing aircraft. Successful helicopter designs are, compared to fixed-wing aircraft, relatively recent innovations. While thousands of monoplanes, biplanes, triplanes, bombers, scouts and fighter aircraft were being produced in World War I, helicopters were not developed in a concerted manner, and then only in a limited manner, until World War II.

From novel, unstable and frightening machines, helicopters have been developed to become incredibly sophisticated flying machines that can fly forward, backward, sideways and, of course, hover. If the military were initially slow to appreciate the potential of helicopters, they have been making up for that short-sightedness ever since. Helicopters have been developed for an incredible variety of military roles, including minesweeping, reconnaissance, rescue, casualty evacuation, gunship, tank-busting, anti-submarine warfare and heavy lifting. The helicopter has also been armed with guns and missiles, and even equipped to carry nuclear depth charges. The military troop-carrying role is among its most important, and the machine's unique capability enables military commanders to insert combat-ready troops into battle.

The civilian uses of the helicopter are no less impressive, and include firefighting, rescue, crop-dusting, law enforcement and of course being the transport of choice for the wealthy and famous. According to the American Helicopter Society (AHS), there are over 45,000 helicopters operating in the world today, and over three million lives have been saved by these aircraft in both peacetime and wartime operations since the first rescue at sea in 1944.

LEFT: **The Flettner Fl 282 Kolibri (hummingbird) was among the first helicopters in front-line military service during World War II. This example was captured from the Germans and tested in the US.**

While early designers may have grasped the broad concept of rotary flight, the power to get this kind of machine airborne simply did not exist. As engine technology developed, so did the ability to get designs from the drawing board into the air. Piston engine technology was accelerated during World War I, as was jet turbine technology during World War II.

Early military helicopters were powered by piston engines and gave sterling service, but the introduction of turboshaft engines dramatically boosted the helicopter's performance in terms of endurance and speed.

Better knowledge of aerodynamics, technical developments, computer-aided design and the creation of lightweight composite materials have led to a huge range of advances in helicopter design, which in turn have boosted all-round performance and lifting capability. Avionics and the incredible array of equipment and weapons that can be carried by a helicopter has made the type among the most expensive in the military inventory.

ABOVE: **The Bell OH-58D Kiowa Warrior has a distinctive Mast-Mounted Sight (MMS) above the rotor system.**

Key to flags

For the specification boxes, the national flag that was current at the time of the helicopter's use is shown.

 Canada

 France

 Germany

 India

 Italy

 The Netherlands

 Poland

 South Africa

 Soviet Union

 United Kingdom

 United States of America

The helicopter is a versatile and vital asset in military inventories around the world, and plays a truly unique part in aviation that at the time of the Wright brothers' historic flight could only been predicted by a few true visionaries.

This book is an A–Z directory covering 80 production military helicopters in detail. The origins, development and operation of each type are fully described, and a specification panel gives key performance and dimensional data, including the helicopter's name, country of origin, date first flown, power, armament, size, weight and performance. All the famous manufacturers are featured, including Bristol, Saunders-Roe and Westland from the UK; Bell, Boeing-Vertol, Hiller, Hughes, Kaman, Piasecki, Robinson and Sikorsky from the USA; and Kamov and Mil from Russia; and they are all illustrated with images from archives, museums and private collections.

BELOW: **Tilt-rotor aircraft such as the Boeing-Agusta BA609 combine the advantages of both rotor and fixed-wing aircraft.**

LEFT: **The Fuerza Aerea Argentina (Argentine Air Force) began operating the Alouette II in 1973.**

Aérospatiale SE 3130 Alouette II

The French-built Aérospatiale Alouette II (lark) secured a place in aviation history by being the first production helicopter to be powered by a gas turbine (turboshaft) engine. Originally manufactured by Sud Aviation and later Aérospatiale, the Alouette II was a sound and successful design that was supplied to the armed forces of 47 nations around the world. It was used for an impressive range of military purposes including observation, photo-reconnaissance, rescue and anti-tank missions. For naval operations, homing torpedoes were carried. When production ended in 1975, over 1,500 had been built, including those under licence in Brazil, Sweden, India and the USA.

The SE 3130 was first flown on March 12,1955, and was soon being used to set altitude records. In July 1956, the type achieved widespread publicity for the first helicopter mountain-rescue. The machine's impressive altitude performance made it ideal for this specialized role. The first delivery to the Armée de l'Air (French Air Force) was on May 1, 1956, and 19 were used in action in Algeria by 1958.

The military version was the first helicopter in the world to be armed with anti-tank missiles (Nord SS11). Aircrews thought the Alouette II was pleasant to fly and easy to manoeuvre, and the bubble-type cockpit made the type ideal for the observation role. The open-frame fuselage contributed to performance by keeping empty weight low. The distinctively shaped tail bumper was fitted to protect the tail rotor from damage during take-off and landings.

The turboshaft-powered Alouette II represented a great advance in performance, serviceability and reliability. The West German armed forces purchased 267 examples and the type also served with the Army Air Corps (AAC) in the UK. After years of military service, many of the type were sold on the civilian market.

ABOVE AND LEFT: **The Army Air Corps (AAC) first trialled the type in 1958 due to technical problems with the development of the Westland Scout. Eventually a total of 17 were purchased and designated Alouette AH Mk2.**

Aérospatiale SE 3130 Alouette II

First flight: March 12, 1955
Power: 1 x Turboméca Artouste IIC6 turboshaft
Armament: None
Size: Rotor diameter – 10.2m/33ft 5in
  Length – 9.66m/31ft 9in
  Height – 2.75m/9ft
Weights: Empty – 895kg/1,973lb
  Take-off – 1,699kg/3,746lb (maximum)
Performance: Speed – 185kph/115mph
  (maximum)
  Service ceiling – 3,300m/10,824ft
  Range – 565km/350 miles

Aérospatiale SE 316 Alouette III

The single-engined Alouette III, developed as a successor to the Alouette II, was larger and could carry up to seven passengers and weapons. In addition to production in France, it was also built under licence by Hindustan Aeronautics Limited as the Chetak (horse) in India and Industria Aeronautic in Romania. Assembly was also carried out in Switzerland and the Netherlands.

The SE 3160 prototype was first flown on February 28, 1959, with full-scale production of the SA 316 (later 316A) starting in 1961. The SA 316B, first flown on June 27, 1968, was fitted with an improved transmission driven by the more powerful Turboméca Artouste IIIB, which allowed an increase in maximum take-off weight. Both were produced simultaneously for a time, but the B model was the main production version. Over 1,400 examples of both versions were built before the main production line closed in 1979, although limited production continued in France until 1985. An early demonstration of high-altitude performance came in 1960 when an Alouette III carrying a 250kg/551lb payload was operated in the Himalayas at altitudes of 6,004m/19,698ft.

French Army experience in Algeria indentified the requirement for a fast, well-armed helicopter. The Alouette fitted this criterion by carrying four wire-guided anti-tank missiles. The helicopter was also used in the counter-insurgency role by the Portuguese military during their

ABOVE: **The Alouette III was a larger machine than the SE 3130 and was built with an all-metal monocoque fuselage.** RIGHT: **In 1964, Aérospatiale produced a single prototype of the SE 3164 Alouette-Canon as an experimental gunship armed with a 20mm MG 151 cannon and fitted with hardpoints to carry the Matra SS 10 anti-tank missile.**

colonial conflicts in the 1960s and '70s, and were the first of the type to be armed with a 20mm cannon.

Pakistan deployed the Alouette III in the Indo-Pakistan War of 1971, mainly for liaison and VIP transport. Two were shot down by Indian forces. The crew of a Rhodesian Air Force Alouette III, armed with 20mm cannon and four 0.50in machine-guns, were credited with shooting down a Britten-Norman Islander of the Botswana Defence Force (BDF) on August 9, 1979.

The Venezuelan Air Force retired the Alouette III in the late 1990s. In June 2004, the type was retired from the Armée de l'Air after 32 years of service. Long-time operator the Irish Air Corps retired the Alouette III in 2007 after 44 years of service, during which over 77,000 flying hours were amassed, including 2,882 air ambulance flights and 1,717 search and rescue missions which

saved 542 lives. Argentina purchased 14 for naval operations, and one was used during the invasion of South Georgia, the prelude to the Falklands War of 1982. The last of these was retired at the end of 2010. The Alouette III remains in service with a number of military and civilian operators.

Aérospatiale SE 316 Alouette III

First flight: June 27, 1968 (SA 316B)
Power: 1 x Turboméca Artouste IIIB turboshaft
Armament: Various – anti-tank missiles, 20mm cannon or machine-guns
Size: Rotor diameter – 11.02m/36ft 2in
    Length – 12.84m/42ft 2in
    Height – 3m/9ft 10in
Weights: Empty – 1,143kg/2,440lb
    Take-off – 2,250kg/4,960lb (maximum)
Performance: Speed – 210kph/130mph (maximum)
    Service ceiling – 3,200m/10,500ft
    Range – 480km/298 miles

LEFT: **The SA 315B Lama was built under licence in India by Hindustan Aircraft Limited (HAL), and was named Cheetah when the type entered service with the military. A modified and upgraded version, the Lancer, has been produced by HAL for counter-insurgency and light-attack operations.**

Aérospatiale SA 315B Lama

This special "hot and high" helicopter developed from the Alouette family was originally designed by Aérospatiale in response to a 1968 Indian military requirement for a helicopter that could be operated in inaccessible and demanding conditions. To create the five-seat (including pilot) SA 315B Lama, Aérospatiale strengthened the airframe of the Alouette II and fitted it with the Artouste IIIB turboshaft and the rotor system from the Alouette III. The first flight of the SA 315 prototype was on March 17, 1969, but it was to be two years before the Lama name was officially adopted by the manufacturers.

The Lama is used in a variety of military roles, including transport, liaison, photography, reconnaissance, observation, ambulance (two stretchers and an attendant can be carried) and air sea rescue, for which a 160kg/352lb hoist is fitted.

External loads of up to 1,135kg/2,502lb can also be carried. The skid landing gear is of the universal type and can be fitted with castoring wheels for ground handling and floats for water operations.

The aircraft has an impressive performance, not least the ability to lift loads to high altitudes. In 1969, a Lama landed and took off in the Himalayas at an altitude of 7,500m/24,605ft – the highest ever recorded for any aircraft, not just a helicopter.

The high-profile record-breaking flights and the type's performance led to orders from the Indian military. In 1971, negotiations were completed for Hindustan Aircraft Limited (HAL) to produce the Lama under licence in India, and were designated Cheetah. The first Indian-assembled SA 315B flew on October 6, 1972, with deliveries to the military beginning at the end of the following year. In 1978, Aérospatiale agreed a contract with Helibras for the assembly of the type in Brazil. Given the name Gavião (hawk), this version was also exported to Bolivia.

LEFT: **Two Indian-built HAL Cheetals of No.114 Helicopter Squadron (Siachen Pioneers), Indian Air Force.**

LEFT: **An HAL Cheetal from No.114 Squadron, Indian Air Force, at a forward high-altitude helipad in the remote Ladakh region in northern India.**

LEFT: **The space frame-type fuselage on the Cheetal allows ground crew easy access for servicing or routine maintenance. Note the position of the main fuel tank.** BELOW: **Two HAL-built Cheetal helicopters of the Indian Air Force (IAF) operating from a base at Leh in the eastern Karakoram Range, high in the Himalayas.**

Aérospatiale built 407 Lamas in France before production ceased in 1989. An upgraded variant was developed by HAL in 2006–07 using the Turboméca TM 333-2M2. Known as the Cheetal, the version, in contrast to the conditions for which the original Lama was designed, was developed for Indian Army operations in the Siachen Glacier region in the eastern Karakoram Range of the Himalayas. The territory is the highest battle-ground on earth, and India and Pakistan have been fighting there intermittently since April 1984. At a height of over 6,000m/ 20,000ft, it is site of the highest helipad in the world, built by Indian forces to support a base for troops. An order for 20 Cheetals was placed the Indian Army in early 2010.

Operators of the Lama and licence-built versions have included the People's Air Defence Force of Angola, Argentine Air Force and Army, Bolivian Air Force, Chilean Army, Chilean Air Force, Ecuadorian Army, Namibian Air Force, Nepal Army, Pakistan Army and Togolese Air Force.

On June 21, 1972, Aérospatiale test pilot Jean Boulet flew a Lama to a height of 12,442m/40,820ft, setting an altitude record for helicopters that stands to the present day.

Aérospatiale SA 315B Lama

First flight: March 17, 1969
Power: 1 x Turboméca Artouste IIIB turboshaft
Armament: None
Size: Rotor diameter – 11.02m/36ft 2in
  Length – 12.92m/42ft 5in
  Height – 3.09m/10ft 2in
Weights: Empty – 1,021kg/2,251lb
  Take-off – 2,300kg/5,070lb (maximum)
Performance: Speed – 192kph/119mph (maximum)
  Service ceiling – 5,400m/17,715ft
  Range – 515km/320 miles

Aérospatiale SA 321 Super Frélon

In the 1960s the Super Frélon (hornet) was the largest helicopter produced in Western Europe, and had to compete for sales with US and Soviet manufacturers. The design comes from a requirement by the French military for a multi-role, medium helicopter. Three military variants were proposed: transport, anti-submarine and anti-shipping. Civil versions were also built.

The first version by Sud Aviation was flown on June 10, 1959, but was abandoned so that the design team could work on a larger, more useful aircraft. The US manufacturer Sikorsky

became involved, developing the main and tail rotor systems and the final design. The larger SA 321, later named Super Frélon, was first flown on December 7, 1962. In Italy, the Fiat company worked on the design of the gearbox and transmission, and later manufactured these items for the production helicopter.

The Super Frélon differed from the first design by being built with a watertight hull and outrigger floats for amphibious operation. The prototype aircraft, completed as a troop transport to carry 38 equipped troops or 15 stretcher cases, was used in

July 1963 to set a number of world speed records for large helicopters. The second prototype was completed for naval service and flown on May 28, 1963. This version was the first to enter production. When production ended in France during 1983, a total of 99 had been built.

The SA 321D was first delivered to the Aéronavale (French Navy) in 1966. Some of these were later modified to carry AM 39 Exocet missiles and fitted with a large thimble-shaped nose cone housing the attack radar scanner. The missiles were carried on mountings on both sides of the fuselage. The alternative weapons load of four torpedoes was twice the number carried by a Sikorsky S-61 Sea King. The SA 321G was a dedicated Anti-Submarine Warfare (ASW) version equipped with dipping sonar and search radar.

When the SA 321G was withdrawn from service, those remaining in Aéronavale service were used for transport, search and rescue, and vertical

LEFT: **The People's Republic of China negotiated an agreement with Aérospatiale to build the Super Frélon under licence in China. The aircraft, designated Z-8, is operated by the air force for search and rescue. The navy operates the type in the same role and for anti-submarine warfare. The thimble-shaped nose cone houses a search radar scanner. The Z-8 remains in production.**

replenishment of ships in the French Navy. The last Super Frélon in French military service was retired in 2010.

Sixteen export aircraft, designated SA 321H, were supplied to the Iraqi Air Force from 1977, complete with radar and Exocet missiles. These helicopters were used in the Iran–Iraq war to attack Iranian shipping. The Super Frélon was also sold to the Israeli Air Force (IAF) in the late 1960s, and the type was used

extensively in action as a troop and heavy lift transport. The type was retired from IAF service in 1991.

The People's Republic of China ordered 16 of the SA 321Ja, an improved version of the SA 321J built for the civil market. Deliveries began in 1975 and were completed by 1977. These aircraft were used in naval service for rescue and ASW operations. Later Chinese licence-built machines,

designated Changhe Z-8, were supplied and deployed in the rescue and ASW role. The ASW version was equipped with search radar, dipping sonar and armed with anti-submarine torpedoes. From 2007, the air force acquired a number to operate in the search and rescue role. The Z-8 remains in production and has been upgraded with the latest glass cockpit technology.

Other military operators have included the Imperial Iranian Air Force/ Islamic Republic of Iran Air Force, Libyan Air Force, Libyan Navy, South African Air Force and Zairian Air Force.

LEFT: **The Super Frélon, like the Sikorsky S-61 Sea King, was designed with a watertight lower fuselage and fitted with outrigger floats for stability to allow the aircraft to be landed on calm water during a rescue operation.**

Aérospatiale SA 321 Super Frélon

First flight: December 7, 1962
Power: 3 x Turboméca Turmo IIIc turboshaft
Armament: Torpedoes, AM 39 Exocet missile
Size: Rotor diameter – 18.9m/62ft
 Length – 23.03m/75ft 7in
 Height – 6.66m/21ft 10in
Weights: Empty – 6,700kg/14,775lb
 Take-off – 13,000kg/28,660lb (maximum)
Performance: Speed – 237kph/147mph (maximum)
 Service ceiling – 3,150m/10,325ft
 Range – 632km/1,020 miles

Aérospatiale SA 330 Puma

The Aérospatiale SA 330 Puma was first developed in response to a French Army requirement for an all-weather, day or night tactical helicopter. The type is a twin-engined, medium transport/utility helicopter originally manufactured in France by Sud Aviation. It was the first all-weather helicopter to enter service with the military forces of Western Europe.

The first of two Puma prototypes was flown on April 15, 1965. Six pre-production machines were then built, the last of which was flown in July 1968. The first production Puma flew two months later, and the deliveries to the Armeé de Terre (French Army) began in early 1969.

In 1967, the Puma was chosen for Royal Air Force service, and this led to a joint production arrangement between Aérospatiale and Westland Helicopters Limited to produce components for the Puma and assemble the type for the RAF. Production continued until 1987,

with a total of 697 having been built. The type was widely exported and is still in service around the world. Civil variants were also produced.

The two Turboméca Turmo 3-64 turboshaft engines are mounted on top of the fuselage and forward of the rotor assembly, which is then driven through a main gearbox that transmits engine power via a single main driveshaft. Originally, the main rotor blades were made of light alloy, but after 1976 they were gradually replaced with those of composite construction. The tricycle landing gear is of the semi-retracting type, with provision for emergency flotation gear.

Argentinian forces deployed the Puma during the Falklands War of 1982. Those in Romanian military service (licence-built by IAR) have been armed with anti-tank missiles. The type is also in service with the forces of Chile, Ecuador, Gabon, Indonesia, Kuwait, Lebanon, Malawi, Morocco, Nepal,

ABOVE: **The Westland-built Puma HC Mk1 entered service with the Royal Air Force in 1971.**

Nigeria, Portugal, Spain and Zaire. In 2010, the Armeé de Terre was operating over 80 Pumas, and some 30 remained in service with the Armeé de l'Air (French Air Force).

The Puma HC Mk1 first entered RAF service in 1971 and, as of 2010, over 30 machines remained in front-line service. In 1991, during the first Gulf War, the HC Mk1 was widely used by the RAF on the battlefront. The type can be optimized for both desert and arctic warfare by the fitting of specialist equipment. The Puma is used on the battlefield to facilitate tactical troop and load movement by day or by night. Up to 16 fully equipped troops or up to 2,032kg/4,480lb of freight can be carried either internally or as an under-slung load. In the casualty (CASEVAC) or medical evacuation (MEDEVAC) support role, six stretcher cases can be carried internally.

LEFT: **In 1969, the Royal Air Force ordered 40 SA33E Puma helicopters which were to be built under licence by Westland Helicopters Limited. The first production machine was flown on November 25, 1970. A further eight were procured in 1979. In 2009, the RAF announced that 30 of the type were to be upgraded to HC Mk2 standard, which involved the fitting of the more powerful Turboméca Makila engine, revised cockpit displays and improved avionics.**

Each aircraft is equipped with GPS and an Instrument Landing System (ILS) to enable the aircraft to be navigated accurately and landed at suitably equipped airfields in poor weather conditions. The aircraft is crewed by two pilots, or a pilot and a weapons systems officer, plus a crewman. The pilots are equipped with Night Vision Goggles (NVG) for low-flying missions at night. The Puma defensive equipment includes an integrated radar warning receiver, missile-approach warning system, an infra-red jammer and automatic chaff and flare dispensers. Additionally, two cabin-mounted 7.62mm General Purpose Machine Guns (GPMG) can be fitted.

In September 2009, it was announced that 30 of the type in RAF service were to receive an extensive upgrade to enhance performance and allow operations in the toughest and most demanding conditions. New Turboméca engines will give 35 per cent more power and a 25 per cent improvement in fuel efficiency. This upgrade is expected to extend RAF aircraft service life for a further ten years.

ABOVE: **The RAF operates the Puma primarily as a troop and logistics transport. Note the engine air intakes protected by debris filters which project forwards over the top of the cockpit.**

Aérospatiale SA 330 Puma

First flight: April 15, 1965
Power: 2 x Turboméca Turmo 3-64 turboshaft
Armament: 7.62mm General Purpose Machine Gun (GPMG)
Size: Rotor diameter – 15.09m/49ft 7in
  Length – 18.15m/59ft 7in
  Height – 4.54m/14ft 11in
Weights: Empty – 3,615kg/7,970lb
  Take-off – 7,400kg/16,280lb (maximum)
Performance: Speed – 274kph/170mph (maximum)
  Service ceiling – 5,185m/17,000ft
  Range – 572km/355 miles

LEFT: **A Eurocopter AS 332L2 Super Puma, operated by the Hong Kong Governmental Flight Service (HKGFS), alighting on the landing pad of USS *Mobile Bay* (CG-53), a Ticonderoga-class missile cruiser, during an exercise in the western Pacific.**

Eurocopter AS 332 Super Puma/AS 532 Cougar

The Super Puma first flown September 1978 was essentially a Puma fitted with more powerful engines, composite rotor blades, new avionics, a modified tail and improved landing gear. These were the AS 332B versions, whereas the AS 332M first flown on October 10, 1980, was a stretched and, from 1986, re-engined version.

In 1990, the military Super Puma (the type has also been very successful on the civil market) were designated as AS 532 Cougar Mk I. Suffix letters denote the version: U – Unarmed; A – Armed; C – Short fuselage; and L – Stretched fuselage. The Cougar Mk II series, launched in 1993, are larger and have had an additional fuselage stretch to

allow extra seats to be fitted. The Cougar was designed to provide high performance, low operating cost and high mission readiness through ease of maintenance. Rotors blades are constructed from composite materials giving excellent serviceability, low vulnerability, an unlimited useful life and resistance to salt-water corrosion. Other improvements include a simplified main rotor hub, a modular main gearbox and a high energy-absorption undercarriage.

As a multi-role helicopter, the Cougar can be armed with machine-guns, cannon, rockets and various missiles. The type is in service with many air forces around the world in numerous military configurations, including transport, Combat Search and Rescue (CSAR), anti-shipping armed with the Exocet missile, and attack helicopter.

An experimental surveillance version served with the French military during Operation Desert Storm in the first Gulf War. A Cougar, equipped with specialized radar, was flown on 24 missions and proved the capability of this remarkable configuration. The helicopter, fitted with Thomson-CSF

ABOVE: **An AS 332 Super Puma operated by the Singapore Air Force landing on the deck of USS *Harpers Ferry* (LSD-49) to refuel during a cross-operating exercise.**

Target radar, was operated behind the front line at an altitude of up to 4,000m/13,123ft to survey the battlefield. This radar is designed to scan 20,000sq km in just ten seconds, and is able to monitor the movements of up to 4,000 vehicles at distances of up to 200km/124 miles. The surveillance version (AS 532UL/Horizon) remains in service with the French Army.

Naval versions of the Cougar include the AS 532SC, which can be armed with two Exocet anti-shipping missiles. The ASW version can be identified by the black nose cone housing for the powerful Varan maritime surveillance radar. The aircraft is also equipped with HS312 dipping sonar completing a potent ASW weapons system.

Operational experience gained with Puma, Super Puma and Cougar helicopters led to the development of the EC725 Caracal, unofficially known as the "Super Cougar". The type was introduced in 2005 and is designed for the most demanding missions. A combat-proven multi-role helicopter, the type has been deployed on many battlefronts around the world, including Afghanistan.

The EC725 is powered by two of the latest generation Turboméca Makila 2A1 turboshaft engines driving a five-bladed

ABOVE: **An AS 532 Cougar in service with the Ecuadorian military. Note the aircraft is not fitted with side pods.**

main rotor, allowing a high level of manoeuvrability. The type is fitted with the latest glass cockpit technology and mission-dedicated avionics. The manufacturer claims to have equipped the aircraft with the most advanced autopilot in the world.

The EC725 is suitable for a full range of military missions, including Combat Search and Rescue, tactical transport, and also casualty/medical evacuation operations. The French Air Force has a total of 14 in service, and the EC725 has been deployed to the Lebanon and Afghanistan. The Royal Saudi Air Force also operates the type, and the aircraft is being licence-built in Brazil.

ABOVE: **An EC725R2 Caracal in service with the French Air Force. The aircraft is equipped for inflight refuelling, and is fitted with a 20mm GIAT cannon in each side pod.**

Eurocopter AS 532UL Cougar

First flight: September, 1978 (Super Puma)
Power: 2 x Turboméca Makila 1A1 turboshaft
Armament: 7.62mm machine-gun, two 20mm GIAT cannon
Size: Rotor diameter – 15.6m/51ft 2in
Length – 15.53m/50ft 11in
Height – 4.92m/16ft 2in
Weights: Empty – 4,350kg/10,250lb
Take-off – 9,000kg/19,840lb (maximum)
Performance: Speed – 249kph/155mph (maximum)
Service ceiling – 3,450m/11,319ft
Range – 573km/357 miles

Aérospatiale SA 341 Gazelle

The design that became the Gazelle was developed by Sud Aviation (later Aérospatiale) in the mid-1960s from a requirement by the French Army for a light multi-role helicopter to replace the Alouette. The design was ultimately refined, bore a resemblance to the Alouette II and used some common components. The new all-metal machine was streamlined and had a fully enclosed cockpit with side-by-side seating for two pilots. The type also featured an anti-torque ducted fan in place of a tail rotor. Known as the Fenestron, the fan is less prone to damage or a tail strike during take-off or landing.

The British military expressed an early interest in the type, and this led to a development and production agreement between Aérospatiale and Westland

ABOVE: **The SA 341B was ordered by the British Army Air Corps (AAC) and built under licence by Westland Helicopters. The first of 158 procured was flown on January 31, 1972, and the type entered service as the AH 1 on July 6, 1974.**

being signed in February 1967. This covered aircraft for the French military as well as those for the RAF, Royal Navy and the Army Air Corps.

LEFT: **The HT2 (SA 341C), fitted with a stability augmentation system and a rescue winch, was ordered by the Royal Navy as a training helicopter. The type entered service with the Fleet Air Arm on December 10, 1974.**

fire from Argentine forces, while another was shot down by an Argentine Pucara ground attack aircraft. British Army Gazelles have seen service in Kuwait and Kosovo, and in Iraq as scouts for other attack aircraft.

In the Light Aviation division of the French Army, the Gazelle (SA 342M) is used primarily in the anti-tank role and armed with four HOT missiles. The French have deployed the Gazelle to combat areas on many occasions, including Chad, the former Yugoslavia, Djibouti, Somalia, and the Cote d'Ivoire (Ivory Coast). During the first Gulf War in 1991, French machines were used in action carrying HOT anti-tank missiles in attacks against Iraqi armour. Few Gazelle sorties were flown by the Iraqi forces due to Allied dominance of air space in the region. Kuwaiti Gazelle crews claimed some kills against Iraqi vehicles during the 1990 invasion. Ironically, Iraq had been one of the major export customers for the HOT-capable Gazelle, and made extensive use of this weapons system in the Iran–Iraq war.

In 1982, Syrian forces used the Gazelle in action against Israeli armour and claimed to have destroyed 30 tanks. The type has also been used in action by Lebanese and Moroccan forces.

The prototype SA 340.001 was first flown on April 7, 1967, followed by four pre-production SA 341 aircraft in August 1968. The Westland-built prototype of the AH1 for the British Army was first flown on April 28, 1970. Within a few weeks, an Aérospatiale-built pre-production machine had been used to set three world speed records for helicopters. The Gazelle continued to be used to set and break records, which gave this fast, light helicopter a very high profile, and this ultimately led to export sales for both military and civil versions.

The first production AH1 was flown on January 31, 1972, and a total of 174 were built. The aircraft was fitted with a powerful Nightsun searchlight and radar when it entered service with the British Army in July 1974. Fondly referred to as the "Whistling Chicken Leg" by some British soldiers, the Gazelle has proved an incredibly reliable helicopter for many years. It has been used as an Air Observation Post and for Forward Air Controller, casualty evacuation, liaison, command and control roles. An upgrade enables crew voice control of avionics equipment using standard helmet microphones and intercom. This allows the pilot to control the aircraft's systems without lifting his hands from the flight controls or having to look ahead or at the ground below.

The Gazelle can be flown by one pilot who relies on the speed and agility of the aircraft to evade detection and enemy fire. However, the type is lightly armoured and vulnerable to ground fire – during the Falklands War in 1982, two AAC Gazelles were lost to small arms

Aérospatiale Gazelle SA 343M

First flight: April 7, 1967
Power: 1 x Turboméca Astazou XIVM turboshaft
Armament: HOT anti-tank missile, 7.26mm machine-gun or 20mm cannon
Size: Rotor diameter – 10.5m/34ft 5in
    Length – 11.97m/39ft 3in
    Height – 3.19m/10ft 6in
Weights: Empty – 991kg/2,184lb
    Take-off – 1,900kg/4,188lb (maximum)
Performance: Speed – 260kph/161mph (maximum)
    Service ceiling – 4,100m/13,450ft
    Range – 710km/440 miles

Eurocopter AS 565 Panther

The single-engined Aérospatiale SA 360 Dauphin (dolphin) was developed by Eurocopter to become the twin-engined AS 365 Dauphin 2. The type is one of the most successful helicopter designs and has achieved excellent sales worldwide. The military version is the Eurocopter AS 565 Panther, which has been sold to a number of air arms around the world.

The Panther is a multi-role light helicopter suitable for troop transport, logistic support and medical evacuation. The type is supplied in two main versions – AS 565UB (Army) and AS 565MB (Navy). The Panther was first flown on February 29, 1984, and entered production in 1986. The airframe is of light alloy construction similar to that of the Dauphin, but with a greater use

of composite materials, including extensive use of glass reinforced plastic and Nomex. This allows a stronger, lighter-weight airframe to be built. The infra-red signature of the AS 565 has also been greatly reduced by finishing

BELOW: **The Z-9C is a version of the AS 565 developed and built under licence in China by the Harbin Aircraft Corporation.**

LEFT: **In 1979, the HH-65 Dolphin was selected by the US Coast Guard (USCG) to replace the Sikorsky (S-62) HH-52A Sea Guard, and a total of 99 were ordered for air sea rescue duties. A further seven were ordered in 2003.**

In 1979, the Dauphin was selected by the US Coast Guard to replace the ageing Sikorsky (S-62) HH-52A Sea Guard air sea rescue helicopter. An order for 99 was placed, and was designated HH-65A Dolphin to be used for the Short-Range Recovery (SRR) role. The HH-65A cannot be landed on water, so a rescue swimmer is carried as part of the four-man crew. The aircraft were manufactured in the US by the Aérospatiale Helicopter Corporation, a division of Eurocopter.

the airframe with a coating of special infra-red-absorbing paint. The airframe has a high crash tolerance, and the helicopter at maximum take-off weight of 4,300kg/9,480lb has been tested to withstand a vertical impact from 7m/23ft. The fuel system, fitted with self-sealing fuel tanks, is designed to withstand a 14m/46ft impact.

The AS 565MB naval version is designed for anti-surface vessel warfare, anti-submarine warfare, search and rescue, troop/logistic transport and casualty evacuation. This type is fitted with an ingenious seaborne-landing system to secure the aircraft to a deck

in the roughest of sea conditions. The so-called "harpoon" is a retractable probe mounted on the underside of the helicopter. On landing, it is lowered to engage in a grid on the deck, which automatically secures the head of the harpoon and stabilizes the aircraft. The AS 565M can be armed with a cabin-mounted 20mm cannon, the AS 15 TT anti-shipping missile or the Mk 46 anti-submarine torpedo, and for shallow water attack the Whitehead A244/S torpedo. The aircraft can be equipped for over-the-horizon laser-designated targeting to allow an attack on an enemy vessel from beyond visual range.

In USCG service, the HH-65 is equipped with pre-programmable autopilot capable of guiding the aircraft on an automatic approach to an exact point in the ocean, then establishing it in a stable 15m/49ft hover. The autopilot can also be programmed to fly the aircraft in a precise search pattern. The system greatly reduces crew fatigue during a rescue mission.

In February 2003, following the terror attacks on the US, an Air Defense Identification Zone (ADIZ) was instigated around Washington, DC. Seven new-build HH-65Cs were acquired by the USCG for an "airborne use of force" mission to intercept unidentified light aircraft operating within the restricted air space.

The AS 565 is built under licence in Brazil by Helibras as the HM-1 Pantera (panther), and in the People's Republic of China by the Harbin Aircraft Manufacturing Corporation as the Z-9C.

LEFT: **A marine abseiling down from an AS 565 Panther of the Mexican Navy during a multi-national maritime military exercise.**

Eurocopter AS 565 Panther

First flight: February 29, 1984
Power: 2 x Turboméca Arriel 2C turboshaft
Armament: Various
Size: Rotor diameter – 11.94m/39ft 2in
Length – 13.68m/44ft 10in
Height – 4.06m/13ft 4in
Weights: Empty – 2,380kg/5,247lb
Take-off – 4,300kg/9,480lb (maximum)
Performance: Speed – 296kph/183mph (maximum)
Service ceiling – 2,500m/8,500ft
Range – 875km/540 miles

LEFT: **The South African Air Force (SAAF) operates 27 AgustaWestland A109LUH helicopters in the light transport role. The machine is painted in standard SAAF camouflage with low-visibility markings.**

AgustaWestland AW109E Power

The manufacturer describes the AW109 as "the world's most versatile light twin helicopter". Originally conceived as a single-engined machine for civilian use, the design was the result of extensive market research.

In 1969, the aircraft was redesigned and fitted with two Allison 250 turboshaft engines, and the prototype was first flown on August 4, 1971. Production deliveries of the eight-seat civil version (named Hirundo, but this was later dropped), began in 1975, the same year that the military potential of the design was being assessed. Agusta worked with Hughes to equip the A109 with the Tube–launched Optically-tracked Wire-guided (TOW) missile. Trials proved to

RIGHT: **The A109LUH is the military version of the AgustaWestland AW109 Power. The type is operated by the Swedish Air Force, and the eight machines in service are equipped for Search and Rescue (SAR) duties.**

ABOVE: **The Royal Air Force operates the AW109E Power for VIP flights.**

be very successful and led to the Italian military placing firm orders for two versions – one for the army, the other for the navy.

Belgium ordered scout and anti-tank versions armed with the TOW missile. Argentina was an early export customer, but two of four machines purchased were lost to British military forces when the Falkland Islands were re-taken in 1982. The two captured helicopters continued to be operated by 8 Flight, Army Air Corps in support of Special Air Service (SAS) units until 2008.

The A109K version developed for "hot and high" operations in mountainous regions had more powerful engines, fitted with dust filters to prevent sand and other material being ingested, which could affect performance or mechanical damage.

Forty years after the type had first been flown, the AgustaWestland company is still manufacturing two versions for military service – the AW109E Power and the AW109 LUH light utility helicopter.

The AW109E Power is a cost-effective, high-performance and versatile aircraft allowing a wide range of military missions to be performed. The pilot's workload is reduced by the use of an advanced digital glass cockpit fitted with six liquid-crystal displays and a four-axis digital Automatic Flight Control System auto-coupled to GPS and ILS. Among the operators of the AW109E Power is the Royal Air Force, which operates three of the type, acquired in 2006, for VIP transport and communications flights with No. 32 (The Royal) Squadron based at RAF Northolt in West London.

The AW109 LUH is established as one of the world's best-selling military light-twin helicopter and is suitable for a wide range of military requirements. The LUH is fitted with duplicated hydraulic and mechanical systems, and the robust airframe has excellent ballistic tolerance for maximum safety and survivability in combat conditions. The availability of a wide range of mission equipment

makes the LUH a true multi-role helicopter for all light helicopter roles, including training, transport, MEDEVAC, SAR, maritime patrol, observation and anti-tank. In addition, the LUH can be armed with machine-guns, rocket pods, machine-gun pods, anti-tank and air-to-air missiles.

AgustaWestland AW109E Power

First flight: August 4, 1971
Power: 2 x Pratt & Whitney Canada PW206C turboshaft or 2 x Turboméca Arrius 2K1 turboshaft
Armament: None
Size: Rotor diameter – 11m/36ft 2in
Length – 13.03m/42ft 9in
Height – 3.5m/11ft 6in
Weights: Empty – 2,000kg/3,461lb
Take-off – 3,000kg/6,608lb (maximum)
Performance: Speed – 285kph/177mph (maximum)
Service ceiling – 6,000m/19,600ft
Range – 964km/599 miles

LEFT: **The production version of the Agusta A129 Mangusta (mongoose) was powered by two Rolls-Royce 2-1004D turboshaft engines. An improved version A129CBT (ComBaT) was built and armed with a 20mm M197 Gatling-type cannon. The type was ordered by the Italian Army. Deliveries of the 60 machines began in 1990.**

Agusta A129 Mangusta/AgustaWestland AW129

The concept that led to the first attack helicopter to be designed and produced in Western Europe was initially based on the highly successful Agusta A109 but evolved into an all-new aircraft. The initial design studies were undertaken with (then) West German helicopter manufacturer MBB, as both the Italian Army and the German Army were considering the options for a light observation and anti-tank helicopter. When the research and preliminary design work was complete, MBB withdrew and Agusta carried on alone.

Detailed design work began in 1978, and the A129 prototype was first flown on September 11, 1983. The Italian Army then placed an order for 60 aircraft. Although Spain, the Netherlands and the UK all expressed interest in an improved A129, all decided to purchase either the Eurocopter Tigre or Hughes AH-64 Apache.

RIGHT: **The AgustaWestland T129 is the latest version of the A129 Mangusta, a battle-proven multi-role attack helicopter.**

The machine is fitted with stub wings and can carry an impressive array of weapons. Both cockpits are equipped with multi-function displays to present information from the integrated aircraft management system, and provide navigation data, weapon status, weapon selection and communications. The helicopter is equipped with an automatic terrain-following flight control system

which provides the level of stability essential for precise weapon aiming.

The A129 can be used in the anti-tank, armed reconnaissance, ground attack, and anti-aircraft role. In the anti-tank role, the AGM-114 Hellfire, BGM-71 TOW and Spike-ER missile can be carried. The A129 can also be equipped with 81mm or 70mm Hydra 70 unguided rockets. A three-barrel 20mm

RIGHT: **The AgustaWestland T129 is powered by two LHTEC-T800 turboshaft engines. The type is being assembled under licence by Tusa Aerospace Industries (TAI) in Turkey, and is equipped with avionics designed and manufactured in that country.**

M197 Gatling-type cannon is mounted in a turret under the nose. For the anti-aircraft role, the AIM-92 Stinger or Mistral missile can be carried. The type is also equipped with systems which allow it to be operated day or night in all weather conditions.

Deliveries to the Italian Army began in 1990, and the A129 has been successfully deployed to back UN missions to Macedonia, Somalia and Angola. Three helicopters were flown in Iraq until Italian forces were withdrawn.

In January 2002, AgustaWestland was awarded a contract to upgrade the first 45 aircraft built to the improved multi-role A129 CBT (ComBaT) standard, and the first of these were delivered to the Italian Army in October 2002. The work included fitting a five-blade main rotor, advanced avionics equipment and improved transmission. A new type of countermeasures suite, including missile launch detector and also a new Global Positioning/Inertial Navigation System (GPS/INS), was part of the A129 CBT upgrade. The work was completed in July 2008.

In June 2007, five A129 CBTs were deployed by the Italian Army to Afghanistan as part of Italy's commitment to the NATO-led International Security Assistance Force (ISAF) in the eastern province of Herat against increased threats from Taliban forces. The helicopters were fitted with the SIAP self-protection package that automatically detects and fires flares to defend against attack from a man-portable anti-aircraft missile.

In 2007, it was announced that Turkey had ordered 51 of the type, designated T129, under the attack and tactical reconnaissance helicopter programme.

Tusas Aerospace Industries (TAI) is the prime contractor and is responsible for final assembly. AgustaWestland is the prime airframe subcontractor, and the Turkish company Aselsan is responsible for the electronics equipment. The T129 is powered by LHTEC-T800 turboshaft engines manufactured by Tusas Engine Industries (TEI) under licence from the Light Helicopter Turbine Engine Company (LHTEC), a joint venture between Rolls-Royce and Honeywell. The first T129 was flown on September 28, 2009, and deliveries began in 2012.

The T129 is a powerful all-weather, day or night multi-role attack helicopter with a formidable weapons payload, excellent performance for hot and high conditions, long range, and an endurance of up to three hours.

ABOVE: **The fuselage of the T129 is constructed as a semi-monocoque with an aluminium frame. Some 50 per cent of the airframe assembly is fabricated from composite materials, and is designed to withstand hits from 12.7mm armour-piercing ammunition. The engines are also protected to the same standard.**

AgustaWestland T129

First flight: September 11, 1983
Power: 2 x LHTEC-CTS800-4N turboshaft
Armament: 20mm M179 Gatling-type, BGM-71 TOW missile, 70mm Hydra 70 rocket, AGM-114 Hellfire missile, AIM-92 Stinger or Mistral missile
Size: Rotor diameter – 11.9m/39ft
Length – 12.5m/41ft
Height – 3.4m/11ft 2in
Weights: Empty – 2,529kg/5,564lb
Take-off – 5,000kg/11,023lb (maximum)
Performance: Speed – 278kph/170mph (maximum)
Service ceiling – 4,725m/15,500ft
Range – 510km/320 miles

AgustaWestland AW101 Merlin

The Merlin, as it is known in British, Danish and Portuguese service, is one of the world's most capable medium helicopters. It resulted from a 1977 UK Naval Staff Requirement seeking a new ASW helicopter needed to replace the Westland Sea King in Royal Navy service. By late 1977, Westland started work on design studies to meet this requirement. At the same time in Italy, the Italian Navy and Italian helicopter company Agusta were considering the

replacement of the Agusta-built Sea Kings then in service. Inter-company discussions led to a joint venture agreement between both companies and countries. A joint company, European Helicopter Industries (EHI), was set up to manage the project, by now designated the EH101 – this was changed to AW101 in 2007.

Manufacture began in March 1985 in both Britain and Italy. The first prototype, PP1 (British military serial ZF641), was rolled out at Yeovil on

ABOVE: The AgustaWestland AW101 Merlin has a range of over 1,300km/808 miles and can accommodate 38 passengers or 26 fully equipped troops. The type can also be configured to carry 16 casualties on stretchers. In the logistical transport role, the machine can lift up to 5,080kg/11,200lb of cargo.

April 7, 1987, and after exhaustive ground testing, first flew on October 9 that year. The second pre-production example, PP2, flew in Italy on November 26, 1987. Assembly of the Merlin began in early 1995, and the first production example flew on December 6, 1995.

Powered by three Rolls-Royce/Turboméca gas turbines, the rugged, crashworthy airframe is of modular construction and is composed mainly of conventional aluminium alloy construction with some composite materials in the rear fuselage and tail section. The naval version has powered main rotor blade folding and tail rotor pylon folding. All versions can fly in severe icing conditions, and incorporate triple hydraulic systems, three independent alternators and a gas turbine auxiliary power unit.

LEFT: The AW101 Merlin is in front-line service with the Royal Air Force in Afghanistan. Note the 7.62mm General Purpose Machine Gun (GPMG) mounted in a cabin window.

LEFT: **A Royal Air Force aircrewman leaving an RAF Merlin helicopter at Camp Bastion in Helmand Province, Afghanistan, following a mission.**

The aircraft and its mission system are managed by two computers, linked by dual data buses. All crew stations can access the management computers and can operate the tactical displays, fed by the Blue Kestrel radar. Navigation is state of the art, with ring laser gyros, inertial reference systems GPS, Doppler and radar altimeters. The avionics include a digital flight control system, a glass cockpit with colour Multi-Function Displays and a comprehensive navigation suite for all-weather navigation and automatic flight.

The Royal Navy received its first fully operational Merlin HM.1 in May 1997 for trials, and the type entered service in June 2000. Although the Merlins are primarily employed as anti-submarine helicopters, the Merlin can also participate in surface warfare. It is designed to operate from both large and small ship flight decks, in severe weather and high sea states, by day or night. Overall dimensions are less than those of a Sea King, and when embarked at sea, British examples can operate from any ship with a capable flight deck.

The type entered RAF service, designated Merlin HC.3, in January 2001. It shares the same RTM322 engines as the Royal Navy examples, but the RAF Merlin has two 7.62mm General Purpose Machine Guns (GPMG) converted for the air role, long-range fuel tanks, air-to-air refuelling capability and has double-wheel main landing gear compared to the Navy version with its single wheel main gear.

The Merlin's operational debut came in early 2003, when four Royal Navy aircraft from No. 814 NAS embarked aboard RFA *Fort Victoria* were deployed into the northern Gulf as part of the UK Amphibious Task Group for Operation Iraqi Freedom. With no submarine threat, the helicopters were used in an anti-surface warfare role, protecting against swarm attacks by small, fast inshore attack craft. With no ASW requirement, the aircraft's active dipping sonar (ADS) was removed to free up space in the cabin for an extra eight seats plus racks for four stretchers. A 7.62mm GPMG was also fitted in the forward starboard window, and a semi-automatic cargo release unit for loading and vertical replenishment or air drops.

The first operational RAF deployment of the type was to the Balkans in early 2003, and Merlins also served in Iraq as part of Operation Telic until July 2009, when British Forces withdrew from Iraq.

Other operators include the Italian Navy, Royal Danish Air Force, Portuguese Air Force and Japanese Maritime Self-Defense Force.

RIGHT: **The AgustaWestland AW101 is a versatile helicopter, and is combat-proven. The Royal Danish Air Force is one of a number of export customers, and operates the type in the transport and Air Sea Rescue (ASR) role.**

AgustaWestland Merlin HM.1

First flight: October 9, 1987 (PP1)
Power: 3 x Rolls-Royce/Turboméca RTM322-01 turboshaft
Armament: Torpedoes, sonobuoy or anti-shipping missiles
Size: Rotor diameter – 18.59m/61ft
Length – 22.81m/74ft 10in
Height – 6.65m/21ft 10in
Weights: Empty – 10,500kg/23,149lb
Take-off – 14,600kg/32,188lb (maximum)
Performance: Speed – 309kph/192mph (maximum)
Service ceiling – 4,575m/15,000ft
Range – 925km/574 miles

AgustaWestland AW159 Lynx Wildcat

In June 2006, the UK Ministry of Defence awarded AgustaWestland a contract to deliver to the Royal Navy and Army Air Corps the latest twin-engine multi-role utility aircraft developed from the extremely successful Lynx family of helicopters. The AW159 Lynx Wildcat was designed to meet the requirement for the British Army's Battlefield Reconnaissance Helicopter (BRH), formerly the Battlefield Light Utility Helicopter (BLUH), and the RN's Surface Combatant Maritime Rotorcraft (SCMR).

Described as a major development of the existing Lynx design, incorporating advanced technology and providing increased capability, the Lynx Wildcat has a high level of commonality in airframe, cockpit displays and avionics between the Army and Navy versions. It has more powerful engines, offering increased power, endurance and economy over existing Lynx powerplants. The most notable changes in appearance are a new tail rotor, low-set tailplane and a redesigned larger nose and rear fuselage. The Army version will meet land utility and reconnaissance requirements, including designation of targets, particularly for the Apache, by using a laser target designator and rangefinder. The RN version will be built for naval warfare. The original contract called for 70 helicopters – 40 for the Army and 30 for the Royal Navy. This was reduced to 62 in December 2008 – 34 for the Army and 28 for the Navy.

The manufacturer's designation for the Lynx Wildcat is the AW159, and this is how the helicopter is marketed for export sales. The AW159 provides a unique, significant upgrade in terms of operational capability when compared to other aircraft in its class. The helicopter

ABOVE: **The AW159 is designed to be operated from destroyers, frigates and offshore patrol vessels or corvettes, and can operate in all environments. The navigation suite is based on an integrated Global Positioning System (GPS) inertial system.**

is equipped with a comprehensive, integrated avionics suite, enabling advanced navigation, communication, weapon management and integration.

Mission sensor options offered to customers include the latest technology radar, active dipping sonar for the naval warfare variant, electro-optical imaging and electronic surveillance measures, and also an integrated self-defence suite. The AW159 is built for at-sea operations, and is designed for all environments, including the harshest sea conditions associated with ship-borne operations. The type is equipped with modern systems designed to

LEFT: **The standard Lynx composite main rotor blades are used, but a new type of four-blade tail rotor is fitted to give improved yaw control. The AW159 Lynx Wildcat will have an endurance of approximately 3 hours with standard fuel, and 4½ hours with auxiliary tanks. The machine is armed with two British-built Sting Ray acoustic lightweight homing torpedoes.**

minimize crew workload, increase reliability and for ease of maintenance. The AW159 delivers an advanced day/night, all-weather, network-enabled capability to find, fix and strike maritime targets. The aircraft has the ability to detect autonomously, identify and engage surface, land and sub-surface targets. Armament options include air to surface missiles, torpedoes, depth charges, air to ground rockets, cannon and heavy machine-guns.

The utility version of AW159, in common with the naval version, has a fully marinized airframe and provisions for a range of mission and utility equipment, which enable a true multi-role capability. The helicopter has a spacious cabin with large doors for easy exit and unloading, and is capable of carrying and deploying a wide range of troop, equipment or weapon payloads. Exceptional agility and the proven LHTEC CTS800 turboshaft engines give the AW159 unrivalled "hot and high" performance.

Construction of the first AW159 began in October 2007, and on November 12, 2009, the first machine completed its maiden flight at the AgustaWestland facility in Yeovil.

The most notable changes in appearance compared to earlier Lynx are the new tail rotor and low-set tailplane with fins to improve flying qualities. The redesigned nose and rear fuselage give more space and easier access to avionic units for servicing and removal, so that aircraft down-time is kept to a minimum. Larger cockpit doors have been designed to give improved crew access and, most importantly, easier exit from the aircraft in an emergency.

The Lynx Wildcat entered service with the Army Air Corps in 2014 and the Royal Navy in 2015.

ABOVE: **The type is designed to carry the future Anti-Surface Guided Weapon (Light) being developed by Thales as the Lightweight Multi-Role Missile (LMM). The heavy version of the missile will replace the Sea Skua.**

AgustaWestland Lynx Wildcat

First flight: November 12, 2009
Power: 2 x LHTEC CTS800-4N turboshaft
Armament: Torpedoes, anti-shipping missiles, 7.62mm machine-gun, 0.50in heavy machine-gun, CRV7 rockets
Size: Rotor diameter – 12.8m/42ft
    Length – 15.24m/50ft
    Height – 3.73m/12ft 2in
Weights: Empty – Unknown
    Take-off – 6,000kg/13,228lb (maximum)
Performance: Speed – 291kph/181mph (maximum)
    Service ceiling – 3,050m/10,000ft
    Range – 963km/598 miles

Bell 47 H-13 Sioux

The Bell 47 is acknowledged to be one of the earliest practical helicopter designs to be used for both military and civil operations around the world. The Royal New Zealand Air Force (RNZAF) still had five in their active inventory at the time of writing, 66 years after the prototype was first flown on December 8, 1945.

Originating from an experimental project evaluated by the US Army during World War II, the Bell 47 was

designed by the brilliant Arthur Young. Having experimented with helicopter design alone for 12 years, Young identified and addressed many of the challenges facing designers of the type, but specifically control and stability. Numerous manufacturers turned down the opportunity to see Young and his designs. In 1941, Bell agreed to allow him to build full-scale versions of what had only been produced as models. The resulting Bell Model 30 was

ABOVE: **The Bell 47 was built under licence by Westland Aircraft Limited for the Army Air Corps (AAC) and entered service as the AH 1 Sioux. The type was also produced by Kawasaki in Japan and by Agusta in Italy. Note the skid-mounted wheels in the down position as an aid to ground handling.**

BELOW: **A Bell H-13B Sioux in US Army service. The machine is painted bright orange, the standard colour for a training helicopter.**

LEFT: **Licence-built in the UK by Westland Aircraft Limited, XT151 was one of the first AH 1 Sioux helicopters to enter service with the Army Air Corps. The machine has been preserved and is displayed at The Museum of Army Flying, Middle Wallop, Hampshire, in the south of England.**

evaluated by the US Army and this experimental design led to the Bell 47. In March 1946, the Civil Aeronautics Administration (CAA) issued the Bell 47 with Helicopter Type Certificate H-1.

In 1947, the United States Army Air Force ordered 28 for evaluation, some of which were also delivered to the US Navy for evaluation. US Army production orders followed under the designation Bell H-13B, later named Sioux; this was the first of many helicopters to enter US Army service to be named after a Native American Indian tribe.

The H-13 saw widespread use with the US Army during the Korean War, being used for observation, transport and, most importantly, for casualty evacuation fitted with a stretcher – carrying panniers mounted on each skid. During this conflict, the H-13 was one of the types that proved the military usefulness of the helicopter. Early in the Vietnam War, the H-13 was used for observation duties.

The Bell 47 had a 27-year manufacturing history. Over 5,000 military and commercial machines were built in 20 versions in the US, and under licence by Kawasaki in Japan, and by Agusta in Italy. In the UK, Westland Aircraft Limited built the type for the British military as the AH 1 Sioux and HT 2. The first of these was flown on March 9, 1965. However, the first 50 machines delivered to the British Army were, for contractual reasons, built by Agusta in Italy. The Royal Air Force also operated some as training aircraft with the Central Flying School (CFS).

NASA used a number of the type to allow Apollo astronauts to train for piloting the Lunar Lander spacecraft in preparation for landing on the surface of the moon.

The type was used to set a number of records, including the helicopter altitude record of 5,650m/18,550ft in May 1949. A year later, a Bell 47 was the first helicopter to be flown over the Alps.

BELOW: **The Bell H-13B was used for a multiplicity of roles by many military services around the world. Although simple in design, the machine was nevertheless strong and reliable.**

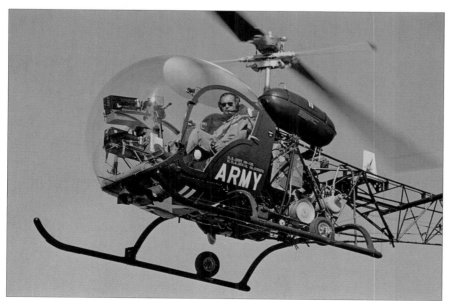

Bell 47 H-13 Sioux

First flight: December 8, 1945
Power: 1 x Lycoming TVO-435-A1A piston engine
Armament: Usually none
Size: Rotor diameter – 11.32m/37ft 2in
    Length – 13.2m/43ft 5in
    Height – 2.83m/9ft 4in
Weights: Empty – 825kg/1,819lb
    Take-off – 1,340kg/2,950lb (maximum)
Performance: Speed – 169kph/105mph (maximum)
    Service ceiling – 3,200m/10,500ft
    Range – 412km/256 miles

Bell UH-1 Iroquois

The Bell UH-1 can rightly be considered as one of the greatest military aircraft of all time. Numerous variants, too many to detail here, were produced, and they served all four arms of the US military, as well as numerous military services around the world.

In 1952, Bell Helicopters responded to a US Army requirement for a medical utility helicopter. Fighting in the Korean

BELOW: **Since the Bell UH-I Iroquois was first flown on October 20, 1956, a total of over 16,000 have been built.**

War was intensifying at this time, and the helicopters deployed there were effectively writing the rule book about the best use of rotary craft in war. Early helicopters, including the Bell H-13 Sioux, were being used, saving countless lives, and by using a larger, higher performance helicopter, even more lives could be saved. It was not obvious to military planners that while the helicopter could move wounded troops away from the front line, the machine could also be used to move fresh troops forward.

ABOVE: **Troops of the 2nd Battalion, 14th Infantry Regiment, 25th Infantry Division boarding a US Army Bell UH-1 Iroquois after an operation in South Vietnam. The UH-1 was known to all service personnel as the "Huey". The name comes from the pronunciation of the original HU-1 (Helicopter Utility) designation, which remains in use today and is the most usual name by which the type is known.**

The Bell-designed Model 204, (first flown on October 20, 1956) had a semi-monocoque metal fuselage and was powered by a single turboshaft engine driving a two-blade main rotor.

On February 23, 1955, the US Army announced its decision, and contracted Bell to build three Model 204 helicopters for evaluation under the designation XH-40.

The US Army finally ordered the helicopter into production (100 aircraft) in March 1960 as the HU-1A Iroquois, which was the first series-built turbine-powered helicopter for the US military. Since that first order, more than 16,000 have been produced worldwide, placing the type among the most commercially successful military aircraft since the World War II. Although the UH-1 offered huge improvements over previous piston-powered helicopters, after flight testing it was concluded that the UH-1A was underpowered. The UH-1B had a more powerful engine and a longer cabin for more passengers or four stretchers, and successful Army trials led to an order for the improved version. This process was to be repeated throughout the service life of this versatile helicopter as improved performance or military requirements drove development.

The US Marine Corps required an assault helicopter to replace fixed-wing and other aircraft, and selected the UH-1B. The machine was navalized by treating the airframe against corrosion. For carrier deck operation,

a brake was fitted to the rotor hub to stop rotation quickly on engine shutdown. A rescue hoist was also fitted. This variant of the helicopter was designated UH-1E.

The very capable UH-1A was deployed to Vietnam, and the first arrived in April 1962 for the CASEVAC role. The transport version arrived in September that year. During the course of the war, the UH-1 went through several upgrades. The short fuselage UH-1A, B and C variants each had

improvements in performance and load-carrying capability. The UH-1B and C served in the gunship role in the early years of the Vietnam War. From 1967, the UH-1B and C gunships were replaced by the new Bell AH-1 Cobra attack helicopter. At the height of the Vietnam War, it was estimated that there could be some 2,000 in the air at the same time. A total of 7,013 were deployed to the South-east Asian conflict and, of these, some 3,305 were destroyed.

LEFT: **The UH-1 Huey will always remain an iconic image of the war in South-east Asia. Since then, the type has been used in many military operations on various battlefronts around the world.**

Bell UH-1B Iroquois

First flight: October 20, 1956
Power: 1 x Avco Lycoming T53-13B turboshaft
Armament: Guns, missiles, grenades and
  rockets projectiles
Size: Rotor diameter – 14.64m/48ft
  Length – 16.15m/53ft
  Height – 3.77m/12ft 5in
Weights: Empty – 2,177kg/4,789lb
  Take-off – 3,856kg/8,483lb (maximum)
Performance: Speed – 204kph/126mph (maximum)
  Service ceiling – 5,790m/19,000ft
  Range – 383km/237 miles

LEFT: **The Bell UH-1H Iroquois is used by the US Air Force for the advanced training of helicopter pilots at the 23rd Flying Training Squadron (FTS), Fort Rucker, Alabama.**

Bell UH-1D/H Iroquois

Bell responded to a US Army requirement for a helicopter to carry more troops into battle by stretching the UH-1 already in US Army service. The manufacturer lengthened the fuselage of a UH-1B model by 1.04m/41in, which was enough space for four more seats, allowing up to 15 troops to be carried. Larger, easy to remove doors were fitted to provide easier access – when troops are being inserted into a hostile location and under fire, the speed with which they can egress an aircraft is vital. Designated the Model 205 by Bell (first flight August 16, 1961), after extensive testing the US Army ordered this new version into production as the UH-1D. Front-line US Army units began to receive the new type in August 1963 and some 2,008 had been delivered by 1966. A total of 2,561 D models were built, including 352 built by Dornier for the then West German armed forces.

As more and more was demanded of the aircraft serving in South-east Asia, in terms of both level of usage and the need for increased carrying capacity, Bell considered how to get more from the design. In 1966, the company trialled

LEFT: **The Fuerza Aerea Boliviana (Bolivian Air Force) was one of the many military force to operate the Bell UH-1H Iroquois. The aircraft is operating during Fuerzas Unidas (United Force), a joint military exercise with US forces.**

the installation of a Lycoming T53-L-13 turboshaft to increase the helicopter's lifting capacity. The US Army approved the design for production, and designated it the UH-1H. This was the version to be produced in the greatest numbers. Deliveries to the US Army began in September 1967, and they received a total of 3,573.

Fuel on the UH-1H was stored in five interconnected self-sealing fuel tanks – two under the cabin floor and three

under the engine to the rear of the cabin. These helicopters did not leave the Bell factory with armour and none was fitted, although armoured pilot seats could be installed.

The large, semi-rigid rotor design used on the UH-1 was a development of that used on earlier Bell helicopters. The two-blade configuration is the reason for the distinctive noise that the type makes in flight, especially when descending to land or turning. The rotor

ABOVE: **A Dornier-assembled UH-1D, one of 325 ordered by the West German government for service with the Luftwaffe.**

blades were fabricated from glass fibre (GRP) but had a metal leading edge. In an emergency, this was strong enough to cut through vegetation while descending into a jungle location.

The final UH-1H built by Bell left the factory in 1986. The type was also built under licence by AIDC in Taiwan and by Agusta in Italy as the AB 205. In Japan, Fuji carried on producing the improved UH-1J into the 1990s. In 2009, the US National Guard (USNG) finally retired the last UH-1 from its inventory.

With more than 16,000 built, the UH-1D/H was produced in greater numbers than any other helicopter in history, and served with some 60 armed forces.

BELOW: **The HH-1H Iroquois was equipped for search and rescue operation. This machine is operated in that role by Detachment 1, 37th Aerospace Rescue and Recovery Squadron (ARRS) from their base at Davis-Monthan, Arizona.**

Bell UH-1D/H Iroquois

First flight: August 16, 1961
Power: 1 x Avco Lycoming T53-L-13 turboshaft
Armament: Guns, missiles, grenades and rockets projectiles
Size: Rotor diameter – 14.63m/48ft
Length – 17.62m/57ft 10in
Height – 4.41m/14ft 6in
Weights: Empty – 2,363kg/5,210lb
Take-off – 4,309kg/9,500lb (maximum)
Performance: Speed – 204kph/126mph (maximum)
Service ceiling – 3,840m/12,600ft
Range – 512km/318 miles

Bell OH-58 Kiowa/TH-67 SeaRanger

The Bell YOH-4 was built to meet a US Navy requirement for an all-metal, four-seat light observation helicopter, and was first flown on December 8, 1962. It was not selected for production. However, Bell went on to develop the design into the widely produced Model 206 JetRanger, the world's most successful turbine-powered light helicopter.

Four years later, this design was chosen by the US Army for observation, scout, and command and control duties to serve alongside the Hughes OH-6 Cayuse. The Bell Model 206A was designated as the OH-58 Kiowa, and over 2,200 were to be built for the US Army. The two-blade, semi-rigid,

all-metal main rotor on the Kiowa differed from the JetRanger by having longer blades. The type was deployed to serve in South-east Asia as soon as it was available in May 1969.
In Vietnam, the OH-58A Kiowa operated with air cavalry, attack helicopter and field artillery units, but this versatile helicopter could also be configured for troop transport, MEDEVAC or for supply missions.

The OH-58A Kiowa was frequently operated with a Bell AH-1G Cobra and would be used to draw enemy ground fire, enabling the crew of the AH-1G to locate the source and attack. The OH-58A was for a time armed with a 7.62mm M134 Minigun mounted

ABOVE: **The Bell OH-58A Kiowa was sold to the Canadian military as the COH-58A (CH-139), and the OH-58B was exported to Austria. A number were assembled in Australia for military service as the 20B-1.**

on the left-hand side of the fuselage, but the resulting vibration when it was fired was too severe for the airframe. Grenade launchers could also be fitted.

Canada also ordered 72 of the type, designated COH-58A Kiowa, later CH-139. The type designated OH-58B was also exported to Austria, and a number were assembled in Australia, as the 20B-1 Kiowa.

The OH-58C was an improved version fitted with a more powerful engine. In 1978, all existing OH-58A machines began to be converted to the same engine and mechanical specification as the OH-58C.

As well as the engine, the OH-58C was equipped with a unique infra-red suppression system mounted on the turbine exhaust to reduce the heat signature, making it difficult for a heat-seeking missile to lock on. This OH-58C was also was equipped for Night Vision Goggles (NVG) capability. Also, it was the first US Army scout helicopter equipped with the AN/APR-39 radar to alert the crew

LEFT: **A US Army Bell OH-58A Kiowa on an observation mission over South Vietnam. The type was first deployed to South-east Asia in 1969.**

when an anti-aircraft radar system locked on to the aircraft. The C-model was also the first to be trial-fitted with an air-to-air missile installation for two AIM-92 Stingers.

From 1998, the US Army began to replace the OH-58C with the more capable OH-58D Kiowa Warrior. In the early 1990s, US Congress decided that the considerable assets of the Army

ABOVE: **A Bell OH-58C Kiowa and a Bell AH-1 Cobra on an artillery spotting and suppression mission. Both are operated by the 19th Air Cavalry of the Hawaii National Guard.**

National Guard (ANG) should be deployed in the war on illegal drugs. In 1992, a total of 76 Bell OH-58As were modified with an engine upgrade, a thermal imaging system, a compatible communications package and improved navigation equipment as part of the Counter Drug Program (CDP).

The US Navy ordered a version of the Kiowa, the TH-57 SeaRanger, as a dual-control, training helicopter. The type is also operated by the US Marine Corps.

In 1993, some 25 years after first ordering the OH-58A Kiowa, the US Army began to take delivery of the TH-67 Creek, a training version of the helicopter.

ABOVE: **A Bell TH-57 Sea Ranger about to land on Helicopter Landing Trainer (HLT) USS Bay Lander (IX-514).** BELOW: **The Bell TH-57 Sea Ranger is flown at NAS Whiting Field-South, Milton, Florida, to provide Advanced Helicopter Training (AHT) for USN, USMC and USCG pilots.**

Bell OH-58 Kiowa

First flight: January 10, 1966 (Bell 206A)
Power: 1 x Allison T63-A-700 turboshaft
Armament: 7.62mm M134 Minigun or 40mm M129 grenade launcher
Size: Rotor diameter – 10.77m/35ft 4in
Length – 12.49m/40ft 11in
Height – 2.91m/9ft 7in
Weights: Empty – 718kg/1,583lb
Take-off – 1,361kg/3,000lb (maximum)
Performance: Speed – 222kph/138mph (maximum)
Service ceiling – 5,800m/19,000ft
Range – 481km/299 miles

Bell OH-58D Kiowa Warrior

This version of the proven and long-serving OH-58 came about as a result of Bell winning the US Army Helicopter Improvement Program (HIP) to produce a comparatively low-cost scout and observation helicopter to support the Hughes AH-64 Apache in combat. Bell's winning design was the OH-58D Kiowa, which was first flown on October 6, 1983.

An upgraded transmission and Allison turboshaft engine housed in an enlarged engine fairing gave the two-seat aircraft the power required for low-level terrain following flight operations. A four-blade main rotor allowed improved performance and reduced noise levels. The distinctive Mast-Mounted Sight (MMS) located on top of the rotor head has TV and infra-red sensors for better target acquisition. The MMS enables the helicopter to be operated in both day and night conditions at the maximum range of the weapons systems and with minimum exposure to an enemy. The helicopter

remains concealed during all but a few seconds of an engagement, then rises to deliver the attack weapons.

A mixed-glass cockpit is a standard fit – computer screens carry all essential flight information but are backed up by analogue flight instruments for emergency use.

The D was conceived as an unarmed scout, but all aircraft were gradually upgraded to Kiowa Warrior status and fitted with offensive weaponry that turned the machine into an attack helicopter. The main difference that distinguishes the Kiowa Warrior from the original D-model is a universal-type weapons pylon to carry AGM-114 Hellfire anti-tank missiles, Stinger air-to-air missiles, 2.75in rockets and a 0.50in M296 heavy machine-gun. The Kiowa Warrior upgrade also featured an improvement in engine power, navigation, communication and survivability (including all-composite rotor blades capable of absorbing direct hits from 0.50in ammunition). Other modifications were made so that the aircraft, after being off-loaded from

LEFT: The D model has a distinctive Mast-Mounted Sight (MMS) assembly above the rotor system, housing TV and infra-red sensors for target acquisition.

LEFT: **A US Army OH-58D Kiowa Warrior in service with the 4th Squadron, 7th Cavalry Regiment, flying below the tree line during an exercise with armoured forces.**

a Lockheed C-130 Hercules, could be assembled, fuelled and armed ready for battle in less than 10 minutes.

Designed to be operated autonomously at stand-off ranges, the Kiowa Warrior is deployed for armed reconnaissance, command and control, day/night target acquisition and designation under all weather conditions. The type can be used to designate targets for precision-guided munitions carried by attack helicopters and other aircraft. Using the Airborne Target Handover System (ATHS), the crew of an OH-58D is capable of rapidly providing ranging information to land artillery or designating targets to other airborne weapons platforms equipped with digital receiving equipment.

The first OH-58D Kiowa Warrior was delivered to the US Army in May 1991, replacing the Bell AH-1 Cobra attack helicopter serving with air cavalry troops and light attack companies. The type also replaced all OH-58A and OH-58C Kiowas in air cavalry units.

The Bell 406CS Combat Scout was based on the OH-58D, and 15 were supplied to Saudi Arabia fitted with a roof-mounted sighting system manufactured by Saab and detachable weapon mountings on each side of the fuselage.

In early 1988, armed OH-58D helicopters were deployed in Operation Prime Chance, to escort oil tankers during the Iran–Iraq War. These operations were primarily reconnaissance flights conducted at night. The US Army used the OH-58D extensively during Operation Iraqi Freedom and Operation Enduring Freedom in Afghanistan.

The OH-58D is considered by some to have the most demanding cockpit workload for the crew of any helicopter in the US Army inventory. The scout/attack role requires much of the flight to involve long periods in the hover at very low altitudes. While the pilot in the right-hand seat flies the aircraft, the crew member in the left-hand seat operates the sighting and other aircraft systems.

The OH-58F is the designation for an upgrade confirmed in January 2011 to extend service life until 2025, more than 50 years after the type first entered service. The changes will include cockpit and sensor upgrades and a nose-mounted targeting and surveillance system replacing the MMS.

LEFT: **An OH-58D from 1st Battalion, 25th Aviation Regiment, on patrol over the city of Baghdad, Iraq.**

Bell OH-58D Kiowa Warrior

First flight: October 6, 1983
Power: 1 x Allison T703-AD-700 turboshaft
Armament: AGM-114 Hellfire missile, Stinger air-to-air missile, 70mm Hydra 70 rockets, 0.50in M296 heavy machine-gun
Size: Rotor diameter – 10.67m/35ft
Length – 12.85m/42ft 2in
Height – 3.93m/12ft 11in
Weights: Empty – 1,492kg/3,829lb
Take-off – 2,495kg/5,000lb (maximum)
Performance: Speed – 237kph/147mph (maximum)
Service ceiling – 4,575m/15,000ft
Range – 555km/345 miles

Bell 209 AH-1 Cobra

Early US military experience in Vietnam identified the urgent requirement for gunship and attack helicopters. Bell had been investigating attack helicopter designs since 1958, and the early design concepts appeared to be very similar to the

BELOW: **The tandem cockpit arrangement was developed to give the AH-1 the narrowest practical frontal aspect, thereby presenting the smallest possible target when approaching the enemy head-on.**

modern perception of an attack helicopter – a stepped, two-seat tandem cockpit in a slim fuselage to reduce frontal area. The US Army instructed Bell to produce a prototype for evaluation, and the Model 207 Sioux Scout was completed in August 1963. While the US Army was impressed by the concept, the 207 was never going to be a fighting aircraft, so they carried on with the search for an attack helicopter. The project was defined as the Advanced Aerial Fire Support

ABOVE: **The AH-1 Cobra was the world's first operational purpose-designed helicopter gunship.**

System (AAFSS) and was eventually won by the Lockheed AH-56 Cheyenne. Although Bell had lost the main attack helicopter project, the design they proposed for the interim combat helicopter was accepted. The Cheyenne project was eventually cancelled in 1972. The very first operational purpose-designed helicopter gunship, the Bell AH-1 Cobra, remains in production.

RIGHT **AH-1G Cobra gunship of the 334th Helicopter Company, 145th Aviation Battalion, flying over Vietnam in 1969.**

Bell rolled out the prototype of the AH-1 on September 3, 1965, and it was first flown on September 7, only six months after being given the go-ahead by the US Army. Bell appreciated the urgency of the requirement as the US military was building an ever-greater presence in South-east Asia and that many US helicopters were being lost to ground fire. The design team chose to use proven mechanical components from the UH-1 Iroquois to save production time, but the slender fuselage was a completely new design. The US Army issued a production contract for a first batch of 110 aircraft given the designation AH-1 (A – Attack; H – Helicopter), and named it Cobra.

The aircraft were produced in record time and were deployed to Vietnam in 1967. Production versions incorporated a number of changes to the prototype. The landing skids, originally designed to be retractable, were removed to save production time and cost, and also to reduce the number of parts that could require servicing or repair.

The AH-1 was the first helicopter designed from the outset to be armed and optimized for combat. Armed with a nose-mounted 20mm cannon and a combination of multiple rocket launchers or 7.62mm Miniguns, the Cobra brought a new dimension to air warfare. Later, in South-east Asia the type was used to attack North Vietnamese armour, and did so with great success while continuing the main role of providing fire support to ground forces and escorting transport helicopters.

Between 1967 and 1973, Bell built 1,110 of the type for the US military, and these accumulated over 1,000,000 operational hours on combat operations, during which some 300 were lost in combat and accidents.

After Vietnam, the Bell AH-1 Cobra remained in service with the US Army as its prime attack helicopter. It was the main weapon to oppose the Soviet tank threat in Europe until replaced in service by the Hughes AH-64 Apache.

The Bell AH-1 Cobra has been exported to the military forces of a number of nations around the world.

BELOW: **A Kawasaki-built AH-1S Cobra in service with the Japanese Self-Defense Force (JSDF).**

Bell AH-1G Cobra

First flight: September 7, 1965
Power: 1 x Lycoming 1 T53-L-13 turboshaft
Armament: 20mm cannon, 7.62mm Minigun pods or 70mm Hydra 70 rockets
Size: Rotor diameter – 13.41m/44ft
Length – 16.26m/53ft 4in
Height – 4.17m/13ft 8in
Weights: Empty – 2,754kg/6,071lb
Take-off – 4,309kg/9,500lb (maximum)
Performance: Speed – 277kph/172mph (maximum)
Service ceiling – 3,530m/11,600ft
Range – 574km/357 miles

Bell AH-1W SuperCobra

The aviation units of the US Marine Corps (USMC) have always had very specific requirements for the type of aircraft in their service. Having seen the impact the helicopter had made during action in Vietnam,

the USMC then evaluated the AH-1G which was in US Army service. In May 1968, the USMC ordered an improved, twin-engine version designated AH-1J and named Sea Cobra. Two engines were required for improved safety

ABOVE: **The AH-1Z Viper is a significantly upgraded version of the AH-1W, fitted with the four-blade rotor system from the Bell Model 609.**

for over-water operations and for improvements in performance, including lift capacity. The power unit chosen was the military version of the Pratt & Whitney Canada T400-CP-400 turboshaft, with the same transmission as used in the Bell UH-1N Iroquois. The USMC also requested an increase in firepower, and specified a 20mm M197 Vulcan-type cannon to be fitted in the nose turret.

In 1971, Iran became the first export customer for the type, and purchased 202 of the AH-1J International model with the more powerful T400-WV-402 engine. Some 70 of these were built to be armed with the Tube-launched, Optically-sighted, Wire-guided (TOW) anti-tank missile. These helicopters were active during the Iran–Iraq war, and reportedly were involved in numerous air combat engagements with Iraqi Mil Mi-8 and Mi-24 attack helicopters. The type remains in service

LEFT: **An AH-1W SuperCobra armed with eight AGM-114 Hellfire anti-tank missiles, two LAU 68D/A pods each carrying seven 70mm Hydra 70 Folding-Fin Aerial Rockets (FFAR), and two chaff/flare dispenser pods. Two AIM-9 Sidewinder air-to-air missiles can also be carried.**

BELOW: **The main armament on an AH-1W SuperCobra is a 20mm M197 three-barrel Gatling-type cannon mounted in a General Electric A/A49E-7 electrically operated turret.**

ABOVE: **An AH-1W SuperCobra from Marine Medium Helicopter Squadron 264 firing against a target during an exercise with ground forces. The machine is carrying an extended-range fuel tank mounted under each wing.**

today, having had been updated with a series of locally manufactured and installed upgrades.

In 1974, the AH-1T was ordered by the USMC as there was a requirement for improved load-carrying capability in high temperatures. This was achieved by installing a more powerful T400-WV-402 engine, driving a new rotor assembly similar to that used on the Bell Model 214 medium transport helicopter.

The AH-1T was fully compatible with the TOW anti-tank missile, as the targeting system and associated sensors were fitted as standard. An improved version known as the AH-1T+ fitted with the T700-GE-700 engines was initially offered to Iran, but negotiation ceased when the Shah of Iran was deposed.

In 1981, when funding was refused to buy a navalized version of the Hughes AH-64 Apache, the USMC instead looked for a more powerful and improved version of the AH-1T. This led to an order for the AH-1W SuperCobra, equipped to carry AIM-9 Sidewinder air-to-air missiles and AGM-114 Hellfire anti-tank missiles. The USMC acquired 179 new-build aircraft and 43 upgraded from existing AH-1T airframes.

By 1996, the USMC were looking for a more capable aircraft but were again refused funding to purchase the

AH-64 Apache. Bell proposed the AH-1Z Viper, a significant upgrade to the AH-1W in service.

On the AH-1Z the stub wings are longer, and each has three mounting points for 70mm Hydra rocket pods, AGM-114 Hellfire anti-tank missile launchers or AIM-9 Sidewinder air-to-air missiles. A Longbow targeting radar pod can be carried on a wingtip mounting.

The AH-1Z Viper is fitted with a composite four-blade main rotor based on that from the Bell 609. This provides improvements in flight characteristics, including an increase in maximum speed, better rate of climb and reduced rotor vibration levels. The AH-1Z was first flown on December 8, 2000, and in 2010 it was confirmed that of the 189 aircraft on order, 58 will be new airframes with

deliveries continuing until 2019. During September 2010, the AH-1Z Viper was declared combat-ready by the US Marine Corps.

Bell AH-1W SuperCobra

First flight: May 8, 1969 (AH-1S)
Power: 2 x General Electric T700-401 turboshaft
Armament: 20mm M197 cannon, 70mm Hydra 70 rockets, 5in Zuni rockets, TOW anti-tank missiles, AGM-114 Hellfire anti-tank missiles, AIM-9 Sidewinder air-to-air missiles
Size: Rotor diameter – 14.6m/48ft
Length – 17.7m/58ft
Height – 4.19m/13ft 9in
Weights: Empty – 4,630kg/10,200lb
Take-off – 6,690kg/14,750lb (maximum)
Performance: Speed – 352kph/218mph (maximum)
Service ceiling – 3,720m/12,200ft
Range – 587km/365 miles

Bell CH-135/UH-1N/UH-1Y

The Bell UH-1 series of military helicopters had been so successful that it was just a matter of time before the type was further and dramatically improved. This came in mid-1968 when the Canadian military, who had recently taken delivery of some UH-1H models, proposed a new version with two turboshaft powerplants instead of the single engine. The resulting

development aircraft, funded by Bell, the Canadian Government and Pratt & Whitney Canada, was the Bell Model 212 which was designed, at this stage, for military use. Pratt & Whitney Canada produced the innovative PT6T Twin-Pac, two turboshaft engines mounted side-by-side driving through a common gearbox to power the rotor. The safety dividend of this arrangement was

ABOVE: **The UH-1Y Twin Huey was built due to a request from the Canadian military for a twin-engined utility helicopter. The machine was powered by the Pratt & Whitney Canada Twin-Pac, two PT6T/T400 turboshaft engines driving through a common gearbox.**

considerable. In the event of one engine failing, a gearbox sensor would signal the working engine to increase output to ensure the continued safe operation of the rotor.

The Canadian Armed Forces (CAF) purchased 50 machines and designated them as the CH-135 after delivery began in May 1971. Bell proposed the type to the US military as the UH-1N Iroquois, and it was procured by the US Air Force. Officially, the UH-1N is known as the Iroquois; inevitably the machine became known as the "Twin Huey". Other early export customers included the air forces of Bangladesh and Argentina. The latter deployed two to the Falkland Islands during the war in 1982, but both were later captured by the British forces.

The Bell Model 212 was sold widely to civilian customers, who were impressed by the performance. Apart from the innovative powerplant

ABOVE: **A Bell Model 212 in Philippine Army service. The type, developed from the Bell Model 205, was the basis for the twin-engined CH-135 (UH-1Y) series of helicopters.**

ABOVE: **Swimmers from the 20th Special Operations Squadron dropping from a distinctively camouflaged Bell UH-1N Iroquois during an open-water training exercise.**

arrangement, the helicopter was very similar to the military UH-1H, and retained the two-blade system.

Agusta built the type under licence in Italy as the AB 212, and developed a unique anti-submarine warfare version armed with torpedoes and missiles for the Italian Navy.

The US Navy and US Marines were the largest operators in the US military. During the invasion of Iraq in 2003, the USMC deployed the UH-1N to provide reconnaissance and communications support to ground troops. These helicopters were also assigned to provide close air support to USMC ground forces during heavy fighting around Nasiriyah in March 2003.

In the late 1990s, the USMC requested Bell to upgrade the UH-1N, and the result is far from a remodelling of the original 1960s design. The Bell UH-1Y Venom, also known as the "Super Huey", is a thoroughly 21st-century fighting helicopter, and is described by the manufacturer as "the legendary Bell UH made better".

This version can be produced by upgrading current machines or be built as new. It has all the effectiveness, safety and reliability of the original UH-1N and, like its predecessor, can operate in the most extreme environments. The UH-1Y is powered by two General Electric T700-GE-401C turboshaft engines which allow a 125 per cent higher payload to be carried, almost 50 per cent increase in range and a higher maximum cruising speed than the UH-1N. The UH-1Y is equipped with a Target Sighting System (TSS), manufactured by Lockheed Martin, to provide target identification in all weather conditions. The UH-1Y is also fitted with an advanced electronic warfare self-protection system which has missile, laser and radar warning receivers, and an automatic countermeasures dispenser.

ABOVE: **A salvo of 70mm Hydra 70 unguided rockets being fired from a pre-production Bell UH-1Y Venom during weapons trials at Fort A. P. Hill, Virginia, USA.**

Bell UH-1Y

First flight: December 20, 2001
Power: 2 x General Electric T700-GE-401C turboshaft
Armament: 7.62mm M134 Minigun, 0.50in heavy machine-gun, 70mm Hydra 70 rockets
Size: Rotor diameter – 14.88m/48ft 10in
Length – 17.78m/58ft 4in
Height – 4.5m/14ft 7in
Weights: Empty – 5,370kg/11,840lb
Take-off – 8,390kg/18,500lb (maximum)
Performance: Speed – 304kph/189mph (maximum)
Service ceiling – 6,100m/20,013ft
Range – 482km/299 miles

Bell CH-146 Griffon

The Bell Model 412 is described by the manufacturer as "the most rugged and reliable medium twin-engine civil helicopter, designed to perform brilliantly in everything, to extreme cold and heat". This versatility and toughness to operate in extremes attracted the attention of the Canadian military when they were considering a replacement for CH-135, OH-58 Kiowa, UH-1 Iroquois and CH-47 Chinook helicopters in the army tactical, observation, rescue and heavy lift roles respectively.

The CH-146 Griffon is the utility helicopter version of the Bell 412 and has the manufacturer's designation of Bell 412CF (CF – Canadian Forces). The Griffon is used for tactical airlift of troops and equipment, logistics, reconnaissance, casualty evacuation (CASEVAC), search and rescue (SAR) missions, and artillery command and control.

The Griffon has served with the Canadian military since 1995, and has played a key role in many national and international humanitarian relief operations, including the 1997 Manitoba Red River flood (Operation Assistance) and the 1988 ice storm (Operation Recuperation) in Canada. In 2004, the type was deployed to Haiti (Operation Halo) to be used in the United Nations relief operations.

The Canadian Army CH-146 Griffon helicopters became part of the Joint Task Force Afghanistan Air Wing (JTFAAW) deployed on Operation Athena. They helped to reduce the risk to ground forces of ambush, land mines and improvised explosive devices (IUD) by providing increased protection to movement of troops by road transport. For air transportation the machine can be partly and quickly disassembled to fit into the Lockheed CC-130 Hercules or Boeing CC-177 Globemaster transport aircraft operated by the Royal Canadian Air Force.

The Griffon has a crew of two pilots (in armoured positions) and a crewman. The cabin has an armoured floor as protection against ground fire, and can accommodate up to ten passengers, eight fully equipped troops or six stretchers.

Although the CH-146 has a maximum gross weight of 5,397kg/11,898lb, the machine has a top speed of 260kph/162mph. Other dedicated military equipment includes missile warning receivers and military radios. The Dillon Aero M134D Minigun was first fitted to eight of the type operating in Afghanistan from late 2008, and these were deployed in a defensive and support role to act as armed escorts for Boeing Vertol CH-47 Chinook helicopters.

The CH-146 Griffon is assembled at the Bell Canada plant at Mirabel, Montreal. The Pratt & Whitney

LEFT: **A Canadian Forces CH-146 Griffon operating in the search and rescue (SAR) role.**

LEFT: **The Bell 412EP Griffin HAR2 is used as a multi-role helicopter by No. 84 Squadron based at RAF Akrotiri, Cyprus. The squadron operates four aircraft, supplied and maintained by a civilian company, but operated by experienced military aircrews.**

PT6T-3D turboshaft engines are also manufactured in Canada. The aircraft is fitted with 30 different mission kits, including a winch for search and rescue, a searchlight or Forward Looking Infra-Red (FLIR) that can be fitted to make the multi-purpose helicopter mission-specific. The Canadian military procured 100 machines, and the majority serve with tactical helicopter squadrons in the Utility Transport Tactical Helicopter (UTTH) role around Canada and overseas. Others are operated as dedicated search and rescue (SAR) helicopters in Combat Support Squadrons (CSS). The last of the type was delivered to the Canadian Forces in mid-1998. In 2005, nine aircraft were sold to a private company contracted to train future helicopter pilots at the Canadian Forces Flying Training School (CFFTS) in Manitoba. As well as military service in Afghanistan, the CH-146 has been deployed to Bosnia and Kosovo, and is expected to continue in service until at least 2021.

The AB 412 Grifone is a version of the Bell 412 built in Italy under licence by Agusta for the Italian Army as a tactical transport.

BELOW: **A CH-146 helicopter providing close air support to Coalition forces on the ground during a clearing operation involving Afghan National Army Commandos and troops of Special Operations Task Force, Kandahar Province, Afghanistan.**

Bell CH-146 Griffon

First flight: 1992
Power: 2 x Pratt and Whitney Canada PT6T-3D Twin-Pac turboshaft
Armament: 7.62mm M134D Minigun or 7.62mm C6 General Purpose Machine Gun (GPMG), 0.50in GAU-21 heavy machine-gun
Size: Rotor diameter – 14m/45ft 11in
Length – 17.1m/56ft 1in
Height – 4.6m/15ft 1in
Weights: Empty – 3,065kg/6,760lb
Take-off – 5,397kg/11,898lb (maximum)
Performance: Speed – 260kph/162mph (maximum)
Service ceiling – 3,111m/10,200ft
Range – 656km/405 miles

LEFT: An MV-22 Osprey from USMC squadron VMM-263 approaching to land on USS *Nassau* (LHA-4), a Tarawa-class amphibious assault ship. For forward flight, the proprotor power nacelles take 12 seconds to rotate to the horizontal position. When the aircraft is operated in the Short Take-Off and Landing (STOL) role, the nacelles are tilted forwards at an angle of 45 degrees.

Bell Boeing V-22 Osprey

The Bell Boeing V-22 Osprey is unique for a number of reasons, but not least because it is the first aircraft designed from the outset to meet the requirements of all four US military services, although to date only the USAF and USMC have taken delivery due to cuts in the US defence budget.

The Osprey is a tiltrotor aircraft which can take off, land and hover like a helicopter. Once airborne, the two propulsion nacelles are rotated forward to convert the machine into a fuel-efficient turboprop fixed-wing aircraft capable of high-speed, high-altitude flight. While offering the vertical take-off and landing (VTOL) advantages of a helicopter, as an aircraft it can fly twice as fast as a helicopter and has a much greater range, resulting in greater mission versatility.

This aircraft's novelty factor is enhanced by a true multi-mission capability for a variety of roles, including amphibious assault, combat support, long-range special operations, transport, MEDEVAC and SAR. The V-22 can be refuelled in flight so can self-deploy (it does not need to be flown in a transport aircraft) and can carry 24 fully equipped combat troops, 9,084kg/20,000lb of internal cargo or up to 6,813kg/15,000lb of external cargo.

The V-22 was first flown in March 1989, and after extensive testing and development which showed that the aircraft met or exceeded required performance parameters, the US Department of Defense approved the Osprey for production in September 2005.

The US Marine Corps, the lead service in type development, has procured the aircraft to perform combat assault and assault support missions. The first Osprey-equipped squadron, VMM-263, was also first of three USMC units to deploy the Osprey in a combat zone in Iraq, October 2007. During May 2009, the type was embarked with the 22nd Marine Expeditionary Unit (MEU), marking the inaugural ship-based deployment of the aircraft. In November of that year, the USMC deployed the type to Afghanistan for the first time.

RIGHT: An MV-22 Osprey being refuelled during a night mission. In November 2009, the USMC deployed the type on offensive operations in Afghanistan.

LEFT: **Two MV-22 Ospreys from USMC squadron VMM-162 preparing to lift off from USS *Nassau* (LHA-4). For stowage aboard ship, the wings are rotated to align with the fuselage. The blades of the proprotors are also folded to reduce space.**

The first offensive combat mission involved the machine being used to insert 1,000 US Marines and 150 Afghan troops into the Now Zad Valley in Helmand Province, southern Afghanistan, to disrupt Taliban communication and supply lines.

The US Air Force is procuring 50 examples of the CV-22, a long-range special operations version, configured for terrain-following, low-level, high-speed flight. Special Operations Command (SOC) received the first operational CV-22 in March 2006, and the first operational unit, the 8th Special Operations Squadron (SOS), was activated at Hurlburt Field in 2007. The type was declared fully operational in March 2009, and by the end of that year the USAF confirmed that the CV-22 was being used on special operations. A CV-22 in USAF service is known to have crashed during a mission in Afghanistan during April 2010.

The United States Navy intends to procure the MV-22 for a variety of maritime roles, including SAR and delivery and retrieval of special warfare teams, along with fleet logistical support.

Production of this complex aircraft is divided between Boeing Rotorcraft Systems and partner Bell Helicopter Textron. Boeing is responsible for the fuselage, landing gear, tail, digital avionics and fly-by-wire flight-control systems. Bell is responsible for the wing, transmissions, rotor systems and engine installation. Final assembly is by Bell at the company's facility in Amarillo, Texas. The 100th aircraft was delivered to the US military in March 2008.

ABOVE AND LEFT: **With twin tail fins and oversized proprotors for an aircraft of its size, the Osprey is very easy to identify in forward flight.**

Bell Boeing CV-22 Osprey

First flight: March 19, 1989
Power: 2 x Rolls-Royce Allison T406/AE1107C turboshaft
Armament: 7.62mm M240G machine-gun, 0.50in M2 heavy machine-gun, 7.62mm GAU-17 Minigun
Size: Rotor diameter – 11.6m/38ft
Wingspan – 25.8m/84ft 7in
Length – 17.4m/57ft 4in
Height – 6.73m/22ft 1in
Weights: Empty – 15,032kg/33,140lb
Take-off – 23,982kg/52,870lb (maximum VTOL);
27,443kg/60,500lb (maximum STOL)
Performance: Speed – 446kph/277mph (maximum)
Service ceiling – 7,620m/25,000ft
Range – 3,890km/2,417 miles

Boeing Vertol CH-46 Sea Knight

In 1960, when Boeing purchased the Philadelphia-based helicopter manufacturer, the Vertol Aircraft Corporation, the company had three types of tandem-rotor helicopter under development. The Vertol CH-46 Sea Knight was in production for the US Navy and US Marines Corps. The aircraft was first flown on April 22, 1958. The first production version was flown on October 16, 1962, and the type has remained in front-line service for over 40 years due to

a series of upgrades. Some 200 of the CH-46E variant will remain in front-line USMC service for the foreseeable future, until a suitable replacement is found. Between 1964 and 1990, over 600 Sea Knight helicopters had been delivered to the USMC and USN.

The USN acquired the HH-46 Sea Knight to lift stores from supply ships to replenish warships of the US Fleet at sea. Equipped with a winch, the machine is also used for SAR duties.

ABOVE: **The CH-46E was a re-engined version of the earlier CH-46A and D models – the upgrade also included self-sealing fuel tanks, protected crew seats and improved avionics. The D model was an A model with improved rotor blades and better engines. In USMC service, the Sea Knight provides all-weather, day or night, assault transport of combat troops, supplies and equipment during amphibious and subsequent operations ashore.**

In contrast, the USMC wanted the Sea Knight as an assault helicopter, to airlift fully equipped troops to and from the battlefront. The fuselage is large enough to accommodate a jeep-type vehicle loaded via a ramp.

The first USMC machine was delivered in 1964 and entered operational service in Vietnam a year later, where the type began to replace the Sikorsky H-34 Choctaw on troop and cargo-carrying duties from US Navy ships in the China Sea. By 1968, the Sea Knight fleet had flown 75,000 hours on 180,000 operations (including

LEFT: **During the US invasion of Grenada, a USMC CH-46 was shot down. Like many helicopters, the type can be vulnerable to small arms fire, but is equipped to deploy flares to confuse heat-seeking missiles.**

ABOVE: **A Canadian Forces CH-113 Labrador landing on the top of Bell Island, a rocky sea stack.**

LEFT: **The CH-113 Labrador was used by the Canadian Forces from 1963 until 2004. This machine is preserved at the Canadian Aviation Museum in Ottawa.**

8,700 missions to rescue wounded USMC personnel) and had carried 500,000 troops.

Known in the USMC as the "Phrog", the Sea Knight has been used in all USMC combat and peacetime deployments. In the first Gulf War (Operation Desert Storm), some 60 US Navy machines were engaged in vertical replenishment (VertRep), supply and CASEVAC duties. During the invasion of Iraq in 2003, CH-46Es of the USMC transported personnel and supplies, including ammunition, to Forward Arming and Refuelling Points (FARP).

The USN retired the HH-46 Sea Knight on September 24, 2004, and replaced it in service with the Sikorsky MH-60S Seahawk. However, the USMC plans to keep the MH-46E in service until it is replaced by the Bell Boeing MV-22 Osprey when this aircraft becomes fully operational.

The Model 107 was also built under licence in Japan by Kawasaki. The first production aircraft was the airliner version, which pre-dated the delivery of the military type by two years. On July 1, 1962, New York Airways put the Model 107-II into service, operating between midtown Manhattan and Idlewild (later Kennedy), La Guardia and Newark airports. When the service was abandoned in the late 1970s, the helicopters were sold to Columbia Helicopters of Aurora, Oregon, for heavy lift and logging operations. One of these machines, built in 1962, was flown for a record 50,000 hours.

Other versions of the CH-46 included the CH-113 Labrador and CH-113A Voyageur, built for the Royal Canadian Air Force and Canadian Army respectively – the Labrador was primarily for search and rescue, while the Voyageur was for the transport of troops and supplies. When the Canadian forces became integrated, both versions were upgraded to a common SAR standard. When the type was retired from Canadian military service, all were purchased by Columbia Helicopters.

Kawasaki-built versions were also exported to Sweden and Saudi Arabia. The US Army evaluated the CH-46 but chose not to procure the type.

ABOVE: **The Boeing Vertol CH-46 Sea Knight has a non-retractable undercarriage.**

Boeing Vertol CH-46 Sea Knight

First flight: April 22, 1958
Power: 2 x General Electric T58-GE-16 turboshaft
Armament: None
Size: Rotor diameter – 15.24m/50ft
Length – 25.7m/84ft 4in
Height – 5.09m/16ft 9in
Weights: Empty – 5,255kg/11,585lb
Take-off – 11,022kg/24,300lb (maximum)
Performance: Speed – 265kph/165mph (maximum)
Service ceiling – 4,300m/14,000ft
Range – 296km/184 miles

Boeing CH-47 Chinook

The Boeing CH-47 Chinook is a twin-engine, tandem rotor transport helicopter that has served with the military forces of 17 nations for over 40 years. The US Army and Royal Air Force are the largest operators of the type.

When this large helicopter first appeared, it was faster than many smaller utility, and even attack, helicopters. With almost 1200 examples built to date, new versions are still in production. Primary roles include troop movement, artillery emplacement and battlefield resupply, and its wide rear loading ramp and three external-cargo hooks means it can carry a lot of cargo or personnel. Despite its age, the Chinook is still among the western world's heaviest lifting helicopters. The wide rear loading ramp and three external-cargo hooks allow heavy payloads to be carried.

The Chinook story began in late 1956 when the US Army announced plans to procure a turbine-powered helicopter to replace the Sikorsky CH-37 Mojave. After much debate, a decision was made to order the Vertol Model 114 under the designation YHC-1B.

ABOVE: **The second largest operator of the Boeing Vertol CH-47 Chinook is the Royal Air Force. At present, the type is operational with the RAF in Afghanistan and Iraq.**

The machine was first flown on September 21, 1961. In the following year it was designated the Boeing CH-47A (Boeing had purchased Vertol in 1962) under the Tri-Service Aircraft Designation System (TSADS).

The Boeing CH-47A Chinook entered US Army service in August 1962, and had a gross weight of 14,969kg/33,000lb. Boeing was keen to increase lifting capacity, and introduced the CH-47B in 1966. The much improved aircraft was fitted with more powerful Honeywell T55-I-7C engines, which allowed an increase in gross weight to 18,144kg/40,000lb. A year later the CH-47C was developed because the US Army had identified a requirement to move a 6,804kg/15,000lb slung load over a distance

LEFT: **The Boeing Vertol YHC-1B (CH-47A) was developed from the Vertol Model 114, and was flown for the first time in 1961.**

RIGHT: **The US Army operated the Boeing Vertol H-1B (CH-47B) in the transport and heavy-lift role. This machine is being used to recover a damaged North American T-2 Buckeye naval training aircraft.**

of 56km/35 miles. Then powered by T55-I-11 engines, the C model had a gross weight of 20,865kg/46,000lb.

The CH-47 Chinook had first been used on combat operations over Southeast Asia in 1965. By 1968, US Army Chinooks had accumulated 161,000 hours of flying time. During the last days of the war, one Chinook is reported to have carried 147 refugees in a single lift.

After the war, Boeing and the US Army began to plan a major fleet upgrade, which led to development of the CH-47D. Some 500 early model Chinooks were extensively modernized by Boeing, and the result was essentially a new aircraft. Boeing completed the first D-model in 1982 and concluded the work in 1994. Only two CH-47Ds were new aircraft which were built to replace US Army losses during Operation Desert Storm.

The CH-47D is a multi-mission aircraft, and is probably the most recognizable transport helicopter in the world. The distinctive twin-rotor configuration allows exceptional handling qualities, enabling the CH-47 to be operated in climatic, altitude and crosswind conditions that typically keep other helicopters on the ground. The CH-47D can be flown at more than 241kph/150mph over

distances in excess of 610km/380 miles when fitted with long-range fuel tanks.

With a flight crew of three, the CH-47D can transport 44 seated troops or 24 stretcher cases. The cabin, which is 9m/30ft 6in in length, can accommodate palletized cargo internally, or a sling load such as a 155mm M198 howitzer externally using a triple-hook system.

The CH-47 Chinooks in RAF service are used primarily for troop and logistical transport, and can carry up to 54 troops or 10,000kg/22,047lb of freight. The cabin is large enough to accommodate two Land

Rover vehicles, while the three external load hooks allow flexibility in the type and number of loads that can be carried. The British Chinook is also used in secondary roles, including SAR and CASEVAC (a total of 24 stretchers can be carried). The aircraft is crewed by either two pilots, or a pilot and navigator and two loadmasters. The aircraft can be armed with up to three M-134 Miniguns or machine-guns.

The Boeing CH-47 Chinook has been in military service with many nations around the world, including Argentina, Australia, Egypt, Iran, Greece, Italy and Japan, as well as with the military forces of Libya, Morocco, the Netherlands, Singapore, Spain, South Korea, Taiwan and Thailand.

ABOVE: **In 1965, the Boeing Vertol CH-47B was deployed to South Vietnam with the 1st Cavalry Division to replace Piasecki H-21 Shawnee helicopters. The type was particularly useful for Pipe Smoke missions to recover downed aircraft.**

Boeing Vertol CH-47D Chinook (US Army)

First flight: September 21, 1961
Power: 2 x Lycoming T-55-GA-712 turboshaft
Armament: 7.62mm Minigun, machine-guns
Size: Rotor diameter – 18.29m/60ft
 Length – 30.18m/99ft
 Height – 5.77m/18ft 11in
Weights: Empty – 10,615kg/24,000lb
 Take-off –22,680kg/50,000lb (maximum)
Performance: Speed – 269kph/167mph (maximum)
 Service ceiling – 2,575m/8,450ft
 Range – 1,207km/748 miles

LEFT: **Crewmen of a US Navy Special Warfare Combatant-Craft (SWCC) attaching their rigid-hull inflatable boat to a CH-47 Chinook during a maritime air transportation system training exercise. Special Forces can increase their range of operation by being transported complete with a boat.**

Boeing CH-47F Chinook

It was inevitable, given the remarkable success of the Chinook, that the manufacturer would seek to develop the type to meet the changing demands of military customers, and extend the life of the design. In July 2007, Boeing announced that it was to begin full-scale production of a new Chinook for the US Army, the CH-47F, all to be remanufactured from existing CH-47D machines.

Developed under the Improved Cargo Helicopter Program (ICHP), the CH-47F completed US Army operational testing in April 2007. The F model is fitted with Honeywell T55-GA-714A turboshaft engines, which allow a top speed of over 315kph/196mph to be attained and an improvement in payload capacity to 9,538kg/21,000lb.

The Chinook fleet is ageing, and the first CH-47Ds reached their designed service life of 20 years in 2002 – it is worth remembering that the D model was remanufactured from earlier A, B, and C models. An ageing helicopter

requires more maintenance per flight hour, and a "new" helicopter was required to keep pace with increases in operational requirements, including cargo capacity and a longer range.

The US Army required their helicopters to link up as part of a battlefield network, and equipped the aircraft with a significantly improved digital communications and situational awareness capability. The primary mission of ICHP, however, remains the

day or night transportation of troops, supplies and equipment in adverse weather, wherever operations are being conducted by US forces.

The ICHP is intended to restore the ageing CH-47D to new condition and extend airframe life by another 20 years for the type to remain in service until 2025–30. Fuselage stiffening to reduce vibration, stress and metal fatigue are being applied to the F model to give an improvement in

RIGHT: **A US Army CH-47F being prepared to lift a 155mm M198 Howitzer of the 101st Airborne Division in training at Fort Benning, Georgia, USA.**

LEFT: **Troops in training preparing to board a CH-47F Chinook at the National Training Center, Fort Irwin, California.** BELOW: **Troops of the US Army's 101st Airborne Division exiting a US Army Boeing CH-47F Chinook in Iraq.**

reliability and therefore lower maintenance and operating costs. The new airframe is manufactured using advanced techniques in which large single-piece components replace conventional sheet metal assemblies and light-alloy honeycomb formers, improving the structural integrity of the aircraft.

The 1970s analogue technology in the cockpit of the CH-47D is replaced with the latest controls and digital displays, including multi-function Liquid Crystal Display (LCD) screens to provide situation awareness for the flight crew through a moving map display with force symbol overlays and electronic messaging. The new systems will also ease cockpit workload and mission planning with the addition of a Data Transfer System (DTS) that allows for the preflight loading and storage of mission data. In addition to making the aircraft a cost-effective and capable digitized tactical platform, the upgrade will cut operation and support costs due to the use of reliable solid-state systems.

Improved air-transportability is an important feature of the CH-47F. Modifications to the aft rotor pylon and internal systems allow for quick removal in preparation for loading into large USAF transport aircraft.

The upgrade has been conceived as what Boeing call "an open architecture system", which allows for future growth

and technology upgrades, including advanced aircraft survivability equipment. Coupled with displays projected in Night Vision Goggles (NVG), the avionics upgrade will greatly improve flight safety at night, especially for challenging external load operations. The new vital avionics is designed to withstand electromagnetic interference and electronic warfare measures. More reliable components that are easier to maintain and repair have been used to improve at-sea compatibility for operations with the US Navy.

The Boeing CH-47F Chinook prototype, the sixth Chinook model designed for the US Army, was first flown at the company's Philadelphia plant on June 25, 2001. Flying the test aircraft from location to location around the US not only proved the aircraft's range capability, but also provided the US Army with an opportunity to conduct trials and assess various operational missions, including desert and mountain conditions.

The US Army is to procure 55 new-build CH-47F models and will have 61 remanufactured to CH-47G standard for use by US Special Forces units. Boeing began CH-47F production in October 2005, and the type was declared combat-ready by July 2007.

By April 2010, a force of 20 of CH-47Fs had been operating for a year in Afghanistan, often flying

up to eight missions per day, every day. This sustained use in a combat environment was used to identify and rectify any technical or maintenance problems with the type.

All Boeing CH-47D Chinooks in US Army service are to be remanufactured as CH-47F models by 2018. The CH-47F has been ordered by Australia, Canada, Italy, the Netherlands and the UK.

Boeing CH-47F Chinook

First flight: June 25, 2001
Power: 2 x Honeywell T55-GA-714A turboshaft
Armament: Various
Size: Rotor diameter – 18.29m/60ft
    Length – 30.18m/99ft
    Height – 5.77m/18ft 11in
Weights: Empty – 10,615kg/23.402lb
    Take-off – 22,668kg/50,000lb (maximum)
Performance: Speed – 315kph/196mph (maximum)
    Service ceiling – 6,100m/20,000ft
    Range – 370km/230 miles

Boeing Vertol MH-47G/E

The MH-47 is the US Army's 160th Special Operations Aviation Regiment (Airborne) (SOAR[A]) long-range, heavy-lift helicopter. Fitted with a probe for air-to-air refuelling, a fast-rope rappelling system and other operation-specific equipment, the MH-47 is used to operate on overt and covert infiltrations, exfiltrations, air assault and resupply missions operations over a wide range of operational conditions. The aircraft can be used for a variety of other missions, including VertRep,

CASEVAC and CSAR. With the use of special mission and night vision equipment, a crew can operate over hostile territory at low altitude, and any terrain in low visibility, with pinpoint navigation accuracy.

Eight CH-47Cs fitted with Night Vision Goggles (NVG) equipment were used by the 160th SOAR(A) from 1981 in the long-range transport role. A further 16 of the CH-47E version equipped with improved navigation, satellite communications and electronic

warfare systems entered service in 1984. The MH-47D, built from the airframe of the CH-47D, entered service in the mid-1980s, but lacked much of the specialized equipment fitted in the MH-47E.

In December 1987, Boeing was contracted to develop and flight-test an MH-47E prototype and then build 25 production aircraft all converted from earlier-model CH-47 airframes. Delivery of the final MH-47E to the 160th SOAR(A) took place in May 1995, having received the first of the type in 1993. The MH-47E Chinook is a modified CH-47D equipped with an integrated cockpit, upgraded Textron Lycoming T55L-714 engines, air-to-air refuelling capability, Terrain Following/Avoidance (TF/TA) radar and upgraded Navigation/Communication (NAVCOM) systems.

Among other modifications is a much greater fuel capacity due to a 3,637-litre/800-gallon auxiliary fuel tank located in the cabin. Boeing-designed sponson-type fuel tanks of honeycomb shell construction are also fitted. The tanks are self-sealing against 12.7mm/0.50in ammunition but can withstand direct hits from larger non-explosive ordnance, even when multiple hits are sustained.

LEFT: **A US Army MH-47G Chinook departing from the USS** *Wasp* **(LHD-1). Note the size of the starboard fuel tank that runs the length of the fuselage.** BELOW: **The MH-47E special operations aircraft is a long-range, heavy-lift helicopter, which is equipped with aerial refuelling capability, a fast-rope rappelling system and other upgrades of operations-specific equipment.**

The MH-47E has a glass cockpit in which display screens have replaced the many instruments. Flying a helicopter on special operations over hostile territory in darkness and poor weather is a high workload occupation, and digital displays are proven to present key information in the most accessible way. An Integrated Avionics System (IAS) permits global communications and navigation, and is the most advanced system of its kind ever installed in a US military helicopter. The IAS includes Forward Looking Infra-Red (FLIR) and Multi-Mode Radar (MMR).

A key US Army operational requirement was that the avionics systems on MH-47E Chinook and MH-60K Pave Hawk helicopters were interchangeable. Crucial equipment such as radios, mission computers and multifunction displays could be exchanged between the types in a few minutes.

In 1991, the type was deployed to Iraq during Operation Desert Storm. Missions included providing ground refuelling for a force of Sikorsky MH-53 Pave Low and Hughes AH-64A Apache helicopters deployed for CSAR duties.

In the first six months, CH-47Es of the US Army flew some 2,000 hours on 200 combat missions. Over 70 of these involved the infiltration or extraction of forces from enemy territory. These missions of up to 15 hours duration were flown at altitudes of up to 4,880m/16,000ft, and crews had to use oxygen. The MH-47E is the only helicopter in the US Army inventory capable of supporting special operations in such a difficult and challenging environment.

Boeing delivered an upgrade to the MH-47E Chinook, which led to the MH-47G. This included a new cockpit with improved displays and a range of avionics upgrades. The MMR in the MH-47G provides terrain avoidance data to a moving map display, and an improved missile-warning receiver has also been fitted. All existing aircraft will be or have been upgraded to this standard. In March 2007, the MH-47G was deployed to Afghanistan.

Boeing MH-47E Chinook

First flight: September 21, 1961 (prototype)
Power: 2 x Textron Lycoming T55-GA-714 turboshaft
Armament: 7.62mm Minigun, 7.62mm machine-gun
Size: Rotor diameter – 18.29m/60ft
Length – 30.18m/99ft
Height – 5.59m/18ft 4in
Weights: Empty – 12,210kg/26,918lb
Take-off – 24,494kg/54,000lb (maximum)
Performance: Speed – 259kph/161mph (maximum)
Service ceiling – 3,094m/10,150ft
Range – 1136km/705 miles

LEFT: **Army Air Corps (AAC) AH-64 Apache helicopters on the flight deck of HMS *Ark Royal* preparing to take off for a training mission.**

Boeing AH-64D Apache Longbow

The AH-64D Apache Longbow, which was first flown as a prototype on May 14, 1992, is a significant improvement on what was already a formidable weapons system. With enhanced performance and new avionics, the new Apache was developed as a result of experience gained in Operation Desert Storm, the first Gulf War. The Longbow name attached to the D-model refers to the advanced AN/APG-78 Longbow millimetre-wave mast-mounted Fire Control Radar (FCR) in a housing mounted above the rotor head. The radar rapidly detects, classifies, prioritizes (up to 128 per minute) and locks on to multiple stationary, mobile or aerial targets in adverse weather, fog, dust and smoke. The unique system enables an attack to be made from beyond enemy range, thereby significantly increasing the helicopter's survivability. An integrated Radio Frequency Interferometer (RFI) passively gives identification of, and precise bearing to, threat emitters at long range.

The D-model can be concealed from enemy view, using terrain, trees or buildings for cover, and hover with only the Longbow radar scanner "looking" over the top. Weapons can be launched from this position. The Pilot Night Vision Sensor (PNVS) and Integrated Helmet And Display Sighting System (IHADSS) provide a visually integrated, night and adverse weather piloting system. Flying and weapon aiming information is presented "head-up" to the pilot. The terrain picture from the FCR may also be selected on the IHADSS.

A radio modem integrated with the sensor suite enables the crew of an AH-64D to share targeting data with other D-model crews. This allows the Apache Longbow to be used as a group to attack targets detected by the FCR of a single helicopter.

The aircraft is powered by two General Electric T700-GE-701C turboshaft engines, which provide better performance during combat. The forward fuselage of the aircraft was revised and the cockpit protected by ballistic armour. Airbags are also fitted, to reduce the risk of injury in the event of a crash landing.

RIGHT: **The Apache's permanent weapon is an underslung M230 30mm cannon, which is directed either manually or slaved to the helmet of the gunner, who sits in the front crew seat.**

Defensive equipment includes chaff and flare dispensers, as well as laser and radar warning sensors.

Deliveries to the US Army began in 1997, and publicity material from Boeing summed up the capabilities of the AH-64D Apache Longbow by highlighting the statement, "the potential for one attack helicopter regiment to destroy up to 256 targets in less than 5 minutes".

LEFT: **An Army Air Corps (AAC) AgustaWestland AH-64D Apache lifting off from the deck of HMS** Ocean, **a Royal Navy amphibious assault helicopter carrier.**

The US Army ordered 501 original AH-64A aircraft to be upgraded to AH-64D standard to be delivered by August 2006. A total of 42 new-build machines were also ordered and the first were delivered in 2007, followed by an order for a further 96 remanufactured machines.

Export customers acquiring new or remanufactured machines have included Egypt, Greece, Israel, Japan, Kuwait, the Netherlands, Republic of China (Taiwan), Saudi Arabia, Singapore and the UAE.

In July 1995, a licence was agreed to allow AgustaWestland to produce the machine in the UK as the WAH-64 Apache Longbow for the Army Air Corps (AAC), where it is designated Apache AH Mk1. A total of 67 were built between 2000 and 2004. The WAH-64D is powered by two Rolls-Royce/Turboméca RTM322 Mk 250 turboshaft engines, a version of which is used to power the AgustaWestland Merlin. The British Army considers the Apache Longbow to be the most significant battlefield weapon to enter service since the introduction of the tank in 1916.

The AH-64D Apache Longbow has been deployed by the US Army to Afghanistan as part of Operation Anaconda, and also in support of Operation Iraqi Freedom. In Iraq and Afghanistan, both the AAC and Royal Netherlands Air Force (RNAF) have used the type for operations against Taliban insurgents.

ABOVE: **An early AH-64 Apache without the Longbow radar scanner flying over a battery of Royal Artillery 155mm AS90 self-propelled guns. The aircraft is operating as part of the NATO-led Stabilization Force (SFOR) in Bosnia and Herzegovina.**

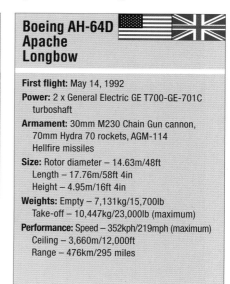

Boeing AH-64D Apache Longbow

First flight: May 14, 1992

Power: 2 x General Electric GE T700-GE-701C turboshaft

Armament: 30mm M230 Chain Gun cannon, 70mm Hydra 70 rockets, AGM-114 Hellfire missiles

Size: Rotor diameter – 14.63m/48ft
Length – 17.76m/58ft 4in
Height – 4.95m/16ft 4in

Weights: Empty – 7,131kg/15,700lb
Take-off – 10,447kg/23,000lb (maximum)

Performance: Speed – 352kph/219mph (maximum)
Ceiling – 3,660m/12,000ft
Range – 476km/295 miles

Bristol Type 171 Sycamore

When the Bristol Sycamore entered Royal Air Force service in April 1953, it became the first British-designed helicopter in British military use. The prototype of the Type 171 was first flown on July 24, 1947, ground running trials having begun earlier in May. In April 1949, the type became the first British-built helicopter to be issued with a certificate of airworthiness, granted so the prototype could be flown to France to be demonstrated at the Paris Salon (Paris Air Show).

The design team for the Type 171 was led by Raoul Hafner, who had been involved in the development and the building of autogyros and gyroplanes in the 1930s. During World War II, he worked at the Airborne Forces Experimental Establishment (AFEE) before joining the helicopter department of the Bristol Aeroplane Company, Filton, near Bristol in 1944.

The Type 171 was very much a helicopter of the time, having a light alloy fuselage. The rotor blades were constructed from spruce and ply ribs fitted to a metal spar and covered with thin plywood. The rotor was to fail dramatically on the second test flight.

The Bristol machine was considerably more streamlined than any Sikorsky helicopter of the period. The Ministry of Supply (MoS) ordered two prototypes which were powered by the US-built Pratt & Whitney Wasp Junior radial engine due to the unavailability of the British-built Alvis Leonides, a sleeve-valve radial piston engine, which was under development. The Leonides engine was fitted in the third prototype, designated Type 171, Mk 2, and first flown on September 3, 1949.

Bristol then built 15 machines (Type 171, Mk 3) with a shorter but wider cabin for evaluation by the British

ABOVE: **One of four Sycamore HC II (Mk 3) aircraft built by Bristol for evaluation by the Royal Air Force for the air sea rescue role. The type entered RAF service in April 1953 as the Sycamore HR14.**

military. Only the RAF ordered the type in quantity, and took delivery of some 90 machines primarily for SAR and light transport duties. The primary RAF version was the Sycamore HR14, modified to position the pilot on the right-hand side of the cockpit.

The Type 171, now named Sycamore, first entered RAF squadron service with Fighter Command. This was because the RAF had numerous fighter squadrons flying from airfields located around Britain, and the prompt rescue of downed aircrew had always

BELOW: **The Federal German government procured 50 Bristol Sycamore Mk52 helicopters for service with the army and navy.**

LEFT: **The Royal Australian Navy obtained three Sycamore Mk 50 helicopters and a further seven HC51s for air sea rescue duties from RAN aircraft carriers. All were powered by the Alvis Leonides sleeve-valve radial piston engine.**

been a problem. The Sycamore was optimized for SAR, meaning that a pilot could be located and rescued from the sea or a mountainside very quickly. The first dedicated SAR squadron was No. 275, based at Linton-on-Ouse, North Yorkshire.

The Sycamore was also deployed overseas for combat in the light assault role, first in Malaya with No.194 Squadron (where the type was to replace the Westland S-51 Dragonfly) and later in Cyprus with No.284 Squadron. It was

the latter unit that worked to develop two key aspects of military helicopter operations – landing troops in difficult-to-reach locations and night flying. In early 1958, a force of some 40 British soldiers were landed from five Sycamores to attack a terrorist position 915m/3,000ft up a mountain south of Nicosia, Cyprus; the British achieved complete surprise due to the use of helicopters. In late 1962, the type was operated in Borneo by No.110 Squadron to transport British troops.

The RAF continued to operate the Sycamore as a front-line helicopter until October 1964, but retained the type for communications duties until mid-1972.

Bristol received export orders for the Type 171 from the military services of Australia, Belgium and West Germany.

As a footnote, British European Airways (BEA) was keen to investigate the commercial opportunities for civil operations, and leased two Type 171s from Bristol. The two machines, designated Mk 3a, had a baggage compartment at the rear of the engine bay. In 1954, BEA operated an experimental passenger service between Southampton, London and Northolt airports. Then, in 1955, a service was inaugurated between Birmingham, Heathrow and Gatwick airports.

ABOVE: **The Royal Air Force ordered 85 of the Sycamore HR14 for the air sea rescue role. Early rescue helicopters in RAF service were equipped with a net to lift a survivor. Later, the rescue strop (sling) was developed, and this is the current method used for recovery operations.**

Bristol Sycamore HR.14

First flight: July 24, 1947
Power: 1 x Alvis Leonides piston radial engine
Armament: None
Size: Rotor diameter – 14.81m/48ft 7in
    Length – 18.63m/61ft 2in
    Height – 3.71m/12ft 2in
Weights: Empty – 1,728kg/3,810lb
    Take-off – 2,540kg/5,600lb (maximum)
Performance: Speed – 204kph/127mph (maximum)
    Range – 531km/330 miles

Bristol Type 192 Belvedere

The Bristol Type 192 Belvedere was a tandem-rotor, twin-engine helicopter operated by the Royal Air Force from 1961 to 1969 for troop transport, supply dropping and CASEVAC. It was the first twin-rotor, twin-engine helicopter and first turbine-powered helicopter to enter service with the RAF.

The Belvedere was developed from the radial-engined Bristol Type 173, first flown on January 3, 1952, which had

been designed for the civil market. When this version was cancelled, Bristol focused on developing the military version, having had interest from the Royal Navy (Type 191), the Royal Canadian Navy (Type 193) and the RAF (Type 192). The prototype of the Type 192 was first flown on July 5, 1958. Three pre-production machines were then delivered to an RAF Trials Unit in October 1960 for evaluation. The type

ABOVE: **The Bristol Belvedere HC Mk1 was designed to meet a Royal Air Force requirement for a medium transport helicopter.**

entered RAF service as the Bristol Belvedere HC Mk1, and a total of 26 were built, with the final aircraft being delivered in June 1962.

The HC Mk1 was powered by two Napier (Rolls-Royce) Gazelle NGa1 turboshaft engines, which allowed sufficient reserve power to allow the aircraft to fly on a single engine even with a full load. The rotor gearboxes were connected by a synchronizing shaft that not only prevented the blades from clashing strike, but also allowed drive to be taken from either engine. The Belvedere could climb at 49m/160ft per minute on one engine.

The first operational unit, No.66 Squadron, was formed in September 1961 after the Belvedere Trials Unit had accumulated a great deal of expertise on the type during the evaluation phase. Based at RAF Odiham, Hampshire, No.66 was part of RAF Transport Command and was equipped with six Belvederes. The other units were Nos.26 and 72 Squadrons.

LEFT: **A short-wheelbase Land Rover Series II and trailer being lifted during crew training at RAF Odiham, Hampshire.**

BRISTOL TYPE 192 BELVEDERE

LEFT: **The Bristol Type 173 was designed as a 13-seat passenger transport and powered by two Alvis Leonides Major radial piston engines. The Type 173 Mk3 was built to evaluate the four-blade rotor system. Note that on this early machine the tailplane is straight, and is fitted with vertical fins.**

In November 1961, two Belvederes from No.66 Squadron were demonstrated during in The Lord Mayor's Show, London, to deliver troops and equipment on to barges moored on the River Thames. In April 1962, a Belvedere of No.72 Squadron demonstrated the type's lifting capability when it was used to deliver the spire to the top of Coventry Cathedral. In the UK, during the severe winter of early 1963, RAF Belvederes were frequently deployed to carry out emergency and supply flights in parts of the country cut off by heavy snow. The type was used for lifting duties as diverse as retrieving a crashed aircraft from a jungle location to transporting the Honest John battlefield missile for the British Army.

Operational experience with the Belvedere stimulated new thinking by military planners for logistical supply and air mobility. It gave commanders on the ground improved battlefield capabilities in the transport of men (18 fully equipped troops or 12 stretcher cases) and cargo (2,725kg/6,000lb internally or 2,385kg/5,250lb slung below the fuselage).

In the eight years that the Belvedere was in front-line service, it was used in Aden, Borneo, Libya, Malaya and Tanganyika (Tanzania). Many of the missions were to deliver British troops directly into combat areas, including jungle clearings.

In March 1969, the last Belvederes in RAF service were retired when No. 66 Squadron was disbanded at RAF Seletar, Singapore.

ABOVE: **In front-line service, all Bristol Belvedere HC Mk1 helicopters were painted in the standard RAF-pattern camouflage of dark green and medium grey. The type could lift an under-slung load of up to 2,385kg/5,250lb.**

Bristol Type 192 Belvedere HC Mk1

First flight: July 5, 1958
Power: 2 x Napier (Rolls-Royce) Gazelle NGa1 turboshaft
Armament: None
Size: Rotor diameter – 14.83m/48ft 8in
Length – 16.56m/54ft 4in
Height – 5.26m/17ft 3in
Weights: Empty – 5,167kg/11,390lb
Take-off – 8,618kg/19,000lb (maximum)
Performance: Speed – 222kph/138mph (maximum)
Service ceiling – 3,050m/10,000ft
Range – 121km/75 miles

Denel AH-2 Rooivalk

The Denel Aviaton AH-2 Rooivalk (kestrel) is a South African-designed and built attack helicopter. Much like the experience that faced US military forces in Vietnam, the South African Defence Force (SADF) was with involved in a conventional war along the country's borders, and defence planners identified a requirement for a dedicated attack helicopter.

In 1984, the Atlas Aircraft Corporation, a predecessor of Denel Aviation, began work on the project, and designed and produced the Atlas XH-1 Alpha test aircraft. The machine was based on the airframe of the Aérospatiale Alouette III and was fitted with the same Turboméca Artouste IIIB turboshaft engine and mechanical components, including

ABOVE: **The Denel AH-2 Rooivalk was purposely designed for operations in the demanding terrain of South Africa's border regions.**

the rotor system. The cockpit was, however, a new design, and followed the tandem layout as used on the Bell AH-1 Cobra and the Hughes AH-64 Apache. To allow the 20mm cannon to be positioned under the nose of

RIGHT: **The main armament on the AH-2 is the French-built Nexter (GIAT) F2, a 20mm single-barrel cannon fed from a magazine containing 700 rounds of ammunition. The South African Air Force (SAAF) procured 12 of the type, and all machines remaining in service are operated by 16 Squadron from their base at AFB Bloemspruit near Bloemfontein in Free State Province.**

the machine, the aircraft was fitted with a tail-wheel undercarriage. Following a first test flight of February 3, 1985, and successful subsequent testing, the development of a production version was confirmed. Part of this development was the decision to utilize the main rotor and the Turboméca Makila 1K2 turboshaft engine from the Atlas Oryx, an upgrade of the Aérospatiale Puma which had been built in South Africa in the face of a UN arms embargo.

The South African Air Force had been operating helicopters for many years in the hostile conditions of the African bush, and demanded that the new attack helicopter could be operated for lengthy periods without sophisticated support. On operations, the AH-2 Rooivalk can be deployed far from base, only requiring a transport helicopter to carry a basic spares supply for support and a ground crew of four to service the machine.

The machine can also carry air-to-air missiles, the South African-produced Mokopa ZT-6 anti-tank missile and 70mm unguided rockets. For defence, the aircraft is designed to have low audio, visual and infra-red signature, and is equipped with an electronic countermeasures suite as well as chaff and flare dispensers.

The Denel AH-2 Rooivalk can carry up to 2,032kg/4,480lb of weapons. The 20mm gas-operated F2 cannon is controlled by sighting equipment fitted on the helmet of the on-board weapons operator. The machine is fitted with infra-red sensors and TV telescopic viewing sights to allow day and night operations. Other sensors and communication equipment makes the Rooivalk a key intelligence link for command and control, to provide the entire operation with shared real time intelligence, potentially lowering the risk of damage from friendly fire.

In the armed reconnaissance role, the helicopter can be deployed to assess enemy positions using long-range sensors to give early warning of any threats. On tactical missions, the Rooivalk will be used to locate the enemy while avoiding detection, provide command with three-dimensional situational awareness, real-time data and identify friendly or enemy forces. Equipment on the helicopter includes a multi-spectral sighting system, allowing military commanders to gain a true 24-hour real-time awareness of the tactical situation. A fully integrated digital management system reduces cockpit workload for the crew, providing more time for battlefield awareness.

ABOVE LEFT: **A salvo of 70mm Folding Fin Aerial Rockets (FFAR) being fired from an AH-2 during a military exercise.** ABOVE: **The Denel AH-2 Rooivalk was designed to be deployed in a remote environment, and requires only a support helicopter to carry spare parts, ammunition and servicing personnel to operate.**

The Denel AH-2 Rooivalk has been purposely developed for the terrain over which the machine is operated, and in this type of combat environment a well-equipped attack helicopter can act as a true force multiplier for the South African military.

A total of 12 AH-2 Rooivalks were ordered, and the type entered service with No.16 Squadron of the South African Air Force in July 1999.

Denel Rooivalk

First flight: February 3, 1985
Power: 2 x Turboméca Makila 1K2 turboshaft
Armament: 20mm F2 cannon, Makopa ZT-6 anti-tank missiles, 70mm FFAR unguided rockets, air-to-air missiles
Size: Rotor diameter – 15.58m/51ft 2in
Length – 16.39m/53ft 9in
Height – 5.19m/17ft
Weights: Empty – 5,730kg/12,632lb
Take-off – 8,750kg/19,290lb (maximum)
Performance: Speed – 309kph/193mph (maximum)
Service ceiling – 6,100m/20,000ft
Range – 740km/437miles

Eurocopter EC665 Tigre/Tiger

The concept for the Eurocopter EC665 attack helicopter goes back to 1984, when the Cold War was still dominating military planning in the West. Helicopter gunships were mainly very vulnerable modifications of utility helicopters. The governments of West Germany and France therefore issued a requirement for an advanced multi-role battlefield helicopter with enhanced survivability. The successful design came from MBB (Messerschmitt-Bölkow-Blohm) in West Germany and Aérospatiale in France –

subsequently forming Eurocopter. Five prototypes were built, and the first was flown in April 1991. One of the prototypes was completed as an anti-tank variant for the specific West German requirement, and another was built to reflect the French escort helicopter variant.

Full production of the machine (Tiger in German service; Tigre in French and Spanish service) began in March 2002, and the first production Tigre HAP (Hélicoptère d'Appui Protection – support and escort

helicopter) for the French Army was flown in March 2003. Delivery of the type began in September 2003. Within a few months, deliveries began of the UHT (Unterstützungshubschrauber Tiger – multi-role fire support helicopter Tiger) ordered by Germany.

RIGHT: **The Eurocopter Tiger UHT is equipped to carry the 70mm Hydra 70 air-to-ground missile, PARS 3LR fire-and-forget and HOT anti-tank missiles. Four AIM-92 Stinger missiles are also carried for air-to-air combat.**

LEFT: **All Eurocopter EC665 helicopters in service with the armed forces of Australia, France and Spain are fitted with the French-built 30mm GIAT cannon.**

In December 2001, Eurocopter was awarded a contract to supply the Australian Army with 22 examples of the Tiger ARH (Armed Reconnaissance Helicopter) version, which were fully operational by 2012. The Tiger ARH is an upgraded version of the Tiger HAP with uprated MTR390 engines and a laser designator for the AGM-114 Hellfire II anti-tank missiles. The ARH can also be armed with the 70mm Hydra 70 rocket. The Tigers are replacing the Bell OH-58 Kiowa and the Bell UH-1 Iroquois-based Bushranger gunship in service with the Australian Army.

The Spanish Army's 24 examples of the Tigre HAD (Helicoptero de Apoyo y Destrucción – support and attack helicopter) version are almost identical to the HAP, but with more engine power available from uprated MTR390 engines and improved airframe protection from ground fire. The French Army subsequently decided to upgrade most of their HAP helicopters to HAD standard.

Some 80 per cent of the airframe is constructed from components manufactured from Carbon Fibre, Reinforced Polymer (CFRP), which allows a weight reduction of up to 30 per cent over a conventional metal structure. This also produces a very smooth surface for improved aerodynamic performance, and is strong enough to withstand 23mm cannon fire.

The airframe is designed to present a low radar signature and minimal infra-red emissions. The machine is equipped with AN/AAR-MILDS radar, laser targeting, missile warning systems and also a SAPHIR-M chaff and flares dispenser.

The Tiger can be armed with the 68mm SNEB folding-fin rocket, AGM-114 Hellfire missile, 70mm Hydra 70 rocket or Mistral air-to-air missiles. The Stinger anti-aircraft missile can also be carried. The highly accurate and powerful 30mm GIAT30 cannon has set a new standard for helicopter-mounted gun performance – during firing trials a burst of five rounds fired from a range of 1km/ 1.6 miles successfully hit the target.

In July 2009, the French Army began operations in Afghanistan with three Eurocopter EC665 Tigre HAP helicopters, the first active deployment of the type in a war zone. On June 4, 2011, French Army machines operated with AgustaWestland AH-64 Apache Longbow helicopters of the Army Air Corps (AAC) against targets in Libya.

ABOVE: **The MTU/Turboméca/Rolls-Royce MTR390 turboshaft engine and gearbox installation. Note the suppressor fitted to the engine exhaust, which reduces infra-red emissions.**

Eurocopter EC665 Tigre/Tiger

First flight: April 29, 1991
Power: 2 x MTU/Turboméca/Rolls-Royce MTR390 turboshaft
Armament: 30mm GIAT30 cannon, AGM-114 Hellfire missile, Mistral air-to-air missile, 70mm Hydra 70 rocket, 68mm SNEB rocket
Size: Rotor diameter – 13m/42ft 8in
Length – 14m/46ft
Height – 4.32m/14ft 1in
Weights: Empty – 3,060kg/6,746lb
Take-off – 6,000kg/13,228lb (maximum)
Performance: Speed – 315kph/214mph (maximum)
Service ceiling – 3,200m/10,500ft
Range – 800km/497 miles

Eurocopter AS 550 Fennec

The Eurocopter (formerly Aérospatiale) AS 550 Fennec (named after the fennec fox) is a lightweight helicopter used extensively by the French Army and Navy, as well as the navies of Argentina and Malaysia, for reconnaissance, attack and other missions. Both the single engine and twin-engine models have also been ordered by Brazil, Columbia, Denmark, Ecuador, Pakistan and Mexico for use as armed scouts and anti-tank helicopters, as well as naval or training aircraft.

There are four single-engined and 11 twin-engined variants, from a basic transport version to a military version armed with a 20mm GIAT M621 cannon and a range of missiles or rockets. It can also be fitted with torpedoes and rockets in naval service. The type first entered service in 1990 and was built by

ABOVE: **The Royal Danish Air Force (RDAF) operates the Eurocopter AS 550 C2 Fennec for liaison duties. A light-attack helicopter, it can be equipped with a pod-mounted 20mm GAU cannon, and the type can be armed with anti-tank missiles.**

Aérospatiale as a development of the AS 350 and AS 355 Ecureuil helicopters. In 1990, the military Ecureuil series of helicopters was renamed Fennec. By 2004, a total of 3,640 aircraft had been

RIGHT: **The Eurocopter AS 350B Ecureuil is operated by the Army Air Corps as a training helicopter. All operations are flown by No.670 and No.705 Squadrons (AAC) from RAF Shawbury, Shropshire, which is also the base for the Defence Helicopter Flying School (DHFS).**

LEFT: **A Eurocopter AS 550 Fennec in service with Brazilian Navy on the flight deck of USS *Pearl Harbor* (LSD-52) during an exercise off the coast of Argentina.**

delivered. The worldwide appeal of the type is due to its versatility and performance. With a maximum ceiling of 7,000m/22,965ft and a mission range of over 645km/348 miles, the Fennec family of helicopters meets the requirements of many civil and military operators.

The latest variant is the AS 550 C3, which has improved protection as it is fitted with self-sealing fuel tanks, energy-absorbing passenger seats and armour protection to the crew seats. If the main gearbox is damaged, it can be run for 45 minutes without lubricant. The rotor blades and hub are designed to be resistant to impact and hits from 7.62mm ammunition. Sophisticated equipment includes a laser and radar warning system, a missile launch detection system and a chaff and flares dispenser to confuse the guidance system of a heat-seeking or radar-guided missile.

The use of composite materials to construct the airframe and finishing the fuselage with infra-red reflective paint reduces radar signature. The main rotor is assembled using the fewest possible number of moving parts to minimize wear and servicing, thus reducing the aircraft's time out of service.

The sophisticated avionics suite enables the crew to fly very low-altitude flight plans safely, utilizing the machine's excellent maneouvrability and power reserves from the Arriel turboshaft engine.

ABOE: **The naval version of the Eurocopter AS 550 Fennec can be equipped with search radar, the scanner for which is mounted in a radome under the nose of the aircraft.**

Eurocopter AS 550 C3

First flight: June 26, 1974
Power: 1 x Turboméca Arriel 2B turboshaft
Armament: 20mm GIAT M621 cannon, BGM-71 TOW anti-tank missile, 68mm Brandt rocket, 7.62mm or 12.7mm FNH machine-gun pods
Size: Rotor diameter – 10.69m/35ft 1in
Length – 12.94m/42ft 6in
Height – 3.34m/10ft 11in
Weights: Empty – 1,202kg/2,650lb
Take-off – 2,250kg/4,960lb (maximum)
Performance: Speed – 278kph/178mph (maximum)
Service ceiling – 7,000m/2,2965ft
Range – 645km/348 miles

LEFT: **The UH-72 Lakota is powered by two Turboméca Arriel II turboshaft engines driving a proven hingeless rotor system. This is fitted with advanced technology composite rotor blades which give decreased vibration and noise while enhancing aerodynamic efficiency.**

Eurocopter UH-72 Lakota

The Eurocopter UH-72 Lakota is a military version of the technologically advanced and proven multi-mission Eurocopter EC145 helicopter, which was based on the MBB/Kawasaki BK 117 C1. The UH-72 is built by American Eurocopter, a division of EADS North America. Originally marketed as the UH-145, the helicopter was selected by the US Army as the winner for the Light Utility Helicopter (LUH) programme in June 2006. In October 2006, the manufacturer was awarded a production contract for 345 aircraft. The UH-72 was required to replace Bell UH-1H Iroquois and Bell OH-58A/C Kiowa helicopters in the US Army and Army National Guard (ANG) inventory.

It was quite an achievement for Eurocopter to secure this contract despite very strong competition from Bell and also McDonnell Douglas who, as the losers, protested the decision. In August, the UH-145 airframe was officially designated UH-72A by the Department of Defense (DoD). After a four-month delay, the first UH-72 was delivered on time. On December 12, 2006, a ceremony attended by General Richard A. Cody, Vice Chief of Staff (Army) and Chief Joe Red Cloud of the Oglala Sioux, Lakota nation, was held to name the aircraft. At the event, the first UH-72A was accepted and named Lokata, continuing a long-standing US Army tradition of using the name of a Native American Indian Tribe for each helicopter type to enter service.

The machines are being built at the American Eurocopter facility in Columbus, Mississippi. While US production was being established,

LEFT: **An H-72A of the 121st Medical Company flying over Washington, DC. The unit was the first US military Medical Evacuation (MEDEVAC) unit to receive the helicopter as a replacement for the Bell UH-1H Iroquois.**

LEFT: **On July 18, 2008, the first Eurocopter UH-72 light utility helicopter to enter service with the Army National Guard (ANG) was delivered to the Eastern Aviation Site at Fort Indiantown Gap, Pennsylvania.**

early aircraft were assembled from components manufactured by Eurocopter Deutschland. The 100th Lakota entered service with the US Army in March 2010. By late October 2010, a total of 138 had been completed, and the final aircraft is expected to be delivered by 2017. The UH-72A is equipped with Vehicle and Engine Multi-function Display

(VEMD), a system which integrates and synthesizes flight and mechanical information. Hydraulic, electrical and engine control systems are all duplicated, and a crashworthy airframe adds a high level of safety and survivability to the aircraft.

The UH-7A Lakota is designed for a range of missions, from general support to personnel recovery. Army

National Guard (ANG) units operate the type on counter-narcotics operations. On delivery to the US Army in January 2007, the first helicopters were sent to the National Training Center at Fort Irwin, California, for MEDEVAC missions. Six months later, in June 2007, the US Army Air Ambulance Detachment (AAD) became the first operational unit. A month later, the Training and Doctrine Command Flight Detachment (TDCFC) at Fort Eustis, Virginia, became the second operational unit.

In January 2009, the United States Military Academy at West Point, New York, received two UH-72As for use as VIP transports. In September 2009, the US Naval Test Pilot School (USNTPS) received the first of five UH-72As as the prime training type for the helicopter training and handling programme.

LEFT: **A total of 16 Eurocopter UH-7A Lakota helicopters are assigned to the Military District of Washington, DC, based at Davison Army Airfield, Fort Belvoir, Virginia.**

Eurocopter UH-72A Lakota

First flight: June 12, 1999
Power: 2 x Turboméca Arriel IE2 turboshaft
Armament: None
Size: Rotor diameter – 11m/36ft 1in
  Length – 13.03m/42ft 7in
  Height – 3.45m/11ft 9in
Weights: Empty – 1,792kg/3,950lb
  Take-off – 3,585kg/7,903lb (maximum)
Performance: Speed – 269kph/167mph (maximum)
  Service ceiling – 5,791m/18,000ft
  Range – 685km/426 miles

Hiller OH-23 Raven

The Hiller OH-23 Raven was developed from the civilian Hiller Model 360, a three- to four-seat helicopter and was ultimately operated by 26 military air arms around the world. The OH-23 series became the first helicopter of any type to be approved for 1,000 hours of operation between major overhauls.

Stanley Hiller had developed the small but innovative Hiller 360, only the third helicopter qualified by the Civil Aeronautics Administration (CAA), and his company was rare in that it was the first in the US producing helicopters without military sponsorship. Worldwide marketing led to orders from the French, who ordered the production version, the UH-12, for Medical Evacuation duties in the Indo–China war. The UH-12 proved

its military capability with the French under very difficult jungle conditions, and although Hiller had been urging the US Army to consider the UH-12 for their inventory, it took the outbreak of the Korean War to bring large orders. Hiller Aircraft's production line in Palo Alto, California, was soon delivering a helicopter a day for US Army use on the Korean front line. In US military service, the model UH-12 was designated the H-23 Raven, and it served in utility, observation and CASEVAC roles – for the latter it could carry two stretchers. Within a few years, the H-23 was back in combat, scouting with the US Army in Vietnam. The type remained the US Army's primary helicopter trainer until 1965. By the time production ended in

ABOVE: **The H-23C was the first of the type to be fitted with a goldfish bowl-type canopy over the three-seat cockpit.**

1965, more than 2,000 examples had been built, with around 300 being exported. Hiller developed and improved the design throughout its service.

In October 1962, pilot Lieutenant Colonel John I. Faulkenberry and mechanic Specialist Fifth Class William Harold Canon broke a US Army distance record for flying a helicopter from one point to another. In nine and a half days they flew 4,345km/2,700 miles. The Hiller would only hold enough fuel for about 80 minutes of flying. With an extra 23 litres/5 gallons of fuel in a can on board, the pair made the trip from airport

LEFT: **The Royal Navy purchased 20 ex-USN HT-2E machines designated as the HT Mk1. A further 21 of the Hiller Model UH-12E were procured, and entered RN service as the HT Mk2.**

to airport, but had to stop only twice at civilian petrol stations along the way for high-test fuel.

The H-23A (UH-12A) had a sloping front window and wooden rotor blades, and was used by both the US Army and US Navy. The H-23B (UH-12B) was designed as a primary helicopter trainer and, although similar to the A model, had the option of skids or a wheeled-type undercarriage and was powered by a Franklin 6V4-200-C33 engine. Versions for the Royal Navy (HT Mk1) and the

US Navy (HTE-2) had wheels. The three-seat H-23D (UH-12D) had a larger engine compared to the earlier UH-12C and had the moulded goldfish bowl-type bubble canopy, reminiscent of the Bell 47, and metal rotor blades. The OH-23G was a dual-control version of the D model, while the OH-23F had a lengthened fuselage with four seats. The G model, powered by a Lycoming piston engine, was the most numerous version with 834 built, followed by the OH-23D, of which 348 were built. The Raven

ABOVE: **The Hiller Model UH-12E-4 was fitted with a larger cabin to accommodate four passengers. The type entered service with the US Army as the H-21F Raven. In 1965, all of the type in service were redesignated OH-23.**

could be armed with two 0.30in M37C machine-guns or two 7.62mm M60C machine-guns.

As well as the US Army and US Navy, operators included Argentina, Biafra, Bolivia, Canada (designated the CH-112 Nomad in Army service), Chile, Colombia, Dominican Republic, France, Germany, Guatemala, Indonesia, Israel, Japan, Mexico, Morocco, the Netherlands, Paraguay, Peru, Sri Lanka, Thailand and Uruguay. The Royal Navy used Hiller HT Mk 1 and 2s for many years, operated by No.705 Naval Air Squadron (NAS), who were tasked with basic flying training of all Fleet Air Arm (FAA) helicopter pilots.

ABOVE: **The cockpit on the Hiller H-23 Raven originally had a sloping front. The type was deployed to Korea for service as a light utility, observation and, when fitted with stretcher panniers, for MEDEVAC duties.**

Hiller OH-23D Raven

First flight: April 3, 1956
Power: 1 x Avco Lycoming VO-540-A1B piston engine
Armament: Usually none
Size: Rotor diameter – 10.82m/35ft 6in
Length – 8.53m/28ft
Height – 2.97m/9ft 9in
Weights: Empty – 824kg/1,816lb
Take-off – 1,225kg/2,700lb (maximum)
Performance: Speed – 153kph/95mph (maximum)
Service ceiling – 4,025m/13,200ft
Range – 330km/205 miles

Hughes OH-6A Cayuse

The basic Hughes Model 369 has become one of the most successful light turbine helicopter designs to have ever been built. In 1960, the US Army announced a contest for the design of a new multi-function Light Observation Helicopter (LOH) for transport, escort, attack, CASEVAC and observation missions. Twelve companies took part in the competition, including Bell and Hiller, but the Hughes design was successful not only by meeting the technical specification, but by also being very competitively priced.

In May 1961, Hughes was contracted to build five prototypes, and the first was flown on February 27, 1962. Originally designated as the YHO-6A by the US Army, under the Department of Defense Joint Designation System (JDS) of 1962, the type became the YOH-6A. In service, the OH-6A was named Cayuse, after the Native American Indian tribe from Oregon. Many nicknames were applied to the odd-looking machine, including the "Flying Egg" and "Loach" – the latter a play on the LOH acronym.

In 1967, during the Vietnam War, the type was rushed into front-line service by the US Army to replace the Hiller OH-23 Raven and Bell OH-13 Sioux helicopters. The OH-6A became and remained the prime scouting helicopter for the duration of the conflict. The type played an extensive role during this period, not only acting as an observation aircraft but also as a target-seeker for Bell AH-1 Cobra gunships escorting troop-carrying Bell UH-1 Iroquois. During the conflict, over one in five of all US military helicopters lost due to ground fire, in operational accidents or destroyed by enemy ground action, was a Cayuse. In March 1973, at the end of the Vietnam War, fewer than 430 of the original 1,420 OH-6A Cayuse helicopters delivered to the US military were still in active service. Veteran pilots and ground crew

RIGHT: From 1971, the OH-6A Cayuse was operated by the Royal Danish Army (RDA), until the operation of all military aircraft became the responsibility of the Royal Danish Air Force (RDAF). Many of the 15 machines originally procured remained in service until 2005.

from the war commended the aircraft for being the most manoeuvrable to fly and the easiest to maintain.

By the mid-1970s, the type was no longer being used for front-line military service, and the remaining aircraft were transferred to the Army National Guard (ANG). During this time, the type began to be used by other organizations, including NASA at the Ames Research Centre and Langley Research Center in Virginia.

In 1966, the OH-6 Cayuse was used to set 22 world records for helicopters, including speed and distance over a closed circuit of 227.69kph/141.48mph over 2,000km/1,243 miles. It also set an all-class helicopter distance record by flying non-stop from Culver City, California, to Ormond Beach, Florida – a distance of 3,561km/2,213 miles in 15 hours, 8 minutes.

This high-profile record-setting, together with an impressive combat reputation, generated considerable market interest. In the early 1980s, Hughes Helicopters was taken over by McDonnell Douglas, and the design was developed as the civil MD 500 light utility helicopter series. This included a range of military helicopters, including the MD 500 Defender. The MH-6B Little Bird, also known as "The Killer Egg", and the heavily armed AH-6C attack variant are both in service with the 160th Special Operations Aviation Regiment (Airborne) (SOAR[A]) of the US Army.

BELOW: **The NH-500E was built under licence in Italy by Breda Nardi. The machine is armed with 70mm Hydra 70 rockets carried in pods.**

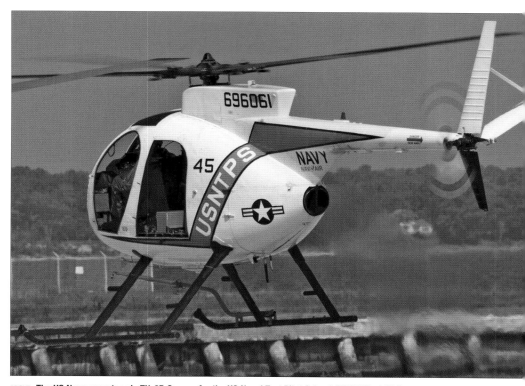

ABOVE: **The US Navy operates six TH-6B Cayuse for the US Naval Test Pilot School (USNTPS) at NAS Patuxent River, Maryland. The aircraft are equipped with instrumentation and avionics to train pilots in all aspects of helicopter handling and performance.** BELOW: **Two US Army AH-6J Little Bird versions taking off for a mission at a forward deployed location in southern Iraq during Operation Iraqi Freedom, 2003.**

Hughes OH-6A Cayuse

First flight: February 27, 1962
Power: 1 x Allison T63-A-5A turboshaft
Armament: 7.62mm XM74 machine-gun or 40mm XM75 grenade launcher
Size: Rotor diameter – 8.03m/26ft 4in
    Length – 9.24m/30ft 4in
    Height – 2.48m/8ft 2in
Weights: Empty – 557kg/1,229lb
    Take-off – 1,090kg/2,400lb (maximum)
Performance: Speed – 241kph/150mph (maximum)
    Service ceiling – 4,875m/15,994ft
    Range – 611km/380 miles

LEFT: A US Army AH-64 Apache ready to be flown from the flight deck of amphibious assault ship USS *Nassau* (LHA-4) during a joint US Army/US Navy exercise in the Atlantic.

Hughes AH-64A Apache

The Hughes YAH-64 was designed to a US Army requirement for an Advanced Attack Helicopter (AAH), and was first flown on September 30, 1975. In 1982, the US Army approved the helicopter, by now designated AH-64A Apache, for production. Deliveries to the

BELOW: An AH-64 Apache armed with 70mm Hydra 70 rockets in pods on the outboard pylons and AGM-114 Hellfire anti-tank missiles on the inner pylons.

US Army began in 1986, and to reduce costs and simplify logistics for the US military, the Apache is powered by the General Electric T700 turboshaft, the same engine that is used to power the Sikorsky UH-60 Black Hawk and the Sikorsky SH-60 Seahawk. The Apache is a large, heavily armed helicopter, but is highly manoeuvrable and a major ground-support asset. The type has been used in virtually every US military action

since entry into service, and has also been exported to Egypt, Greece, Israel (the second largest operator after the US), Japan, the Netherlands, Saudi Arabia and the United Arab Emirates. Between 1986 and 1997, a total of 937 were produced.

Although complex, the Apache is designed for ease of maintenance in the field. The airframe and rotor system is designed to withstand hits from 23mm cannon ammunition, and the cockpit is constructed to withstand a crash impact of up to 13m/42ft per second.

The AH-64 Apache is configured to be operated in day or night conditions, and is fitted with a weapons system capable of identifying and attack the enemy position. The stub wings have hardpoints to carry an array of weapons, including the AGM-114 Hellfire missile designed to destroy a tank at a range of up to 20km/32 miles, pod-mounted 70mm Hydra 70 or 70mm AIM-92 ATAS folding-fin high-explosive rockets. A 30mm M230 Chain Gun cannon is mounted in a hydraulically operated turret under the forward fuselage. The gun, which has a firing rate of 625 rounds per minute, is aimed using helmet-mounted sighting equipment. The Apache is equipped with target-designating sensors to enable other helicopters or tanks to lock on and attack. Other electronic equipment fitted includes navigational

LEFT: **A pre-production Hughes YAH-64 Apache. The four-blade main rotor is manufactured to withstand a hit from 23mm ammunition. The co-pilot/gunner is seated in the front, with the command pilot in a raised position behind. The cockpit area, including glazing, is heavily armoured. All fuel tanks on the aircraft are self-sealing.**

aids, communications and various sensors. As defence from an enemy heat-seeking missile, the engine exhaust gases are cooled by being passed through a system of nozzles, thus reducing the infra-red signature.

The AH-64 Apache is designed to be operated from a forward base close to the battlefront and can be re-armed and refuelled in a short time. The type has a combat radius of just 250km/155 miles.

The US Army first deployed the AH-64A Apache in combat during Operation Just Cause, the invasion of Panama, on December 19, 1989. The type amassed 240 combat hours, mainly on night operations, during this action.

In 1991, at the opening of Operation Desert Storm in the first Gulf War, the first shots fired by Allied forces were from eight AH-64A Apaches deployed on missions to destroy parts of the Iraqi radar-defence network, to allow attacking aircraft undetected access to enemy targets. During the ground war phase, a total of 277 of the type were flown in battle and destroyed many Iraqi vehicles, including over 500 tanks. The Israeli Air Force ordered 42 aircraft, and the first was delivered in 1990.

ABOVE: **The AH-64 Apache is fitted a 30mm M230 Chain Gun cannon in a hydraulically operated mounting. The weapon was designed and developed by Hughes, but is now manufactured by Alliant Techsystems.**

AH-64A Apache

First flight: September 30, 1975
Power: 2 x General Electric T700-GE-700 turboshaft
Armament: 30mm M230 Chain Gun, 70mm Hydra 70 or 70mm AIM-92 Stinger, AGM-114 Hellfire, AIM-9 Sidewinder
Size: Rotor diameter – 14.63m/48ft
Length – 14.97m/49ft 2in
Height – 4.66m/15ft 4in
Weights: Empty – 5,165kg/11,363lb
Take-off – 9,525kg/20,995lb (maximum)
Performance: Speed – 293kph/182mph (maximum)
Ceiling – 6,400m/21,000ft
Range – 250km/155 miles

Kaman H-43B Huskie

Charles Kaman's first helicopter, the K-125A first flown in 1947, was fitted with a patented servo-flap-controlled intermeshing rotor system. The two rotors, mounted on separate pylons tilted outwards, were designed to intermesh while rotating in opposite directions. This innovative design meant that the rotors would generate increased lift while eliminating the requirement for an anti-torque tail rotor. The result was a smaller, mechanically simplified and very stable design.

The K-125A design was developed into the K-190, which was flown a year later. The K-225 was the next development, and came to the attention of the US Navy, who took delivery of two machines in 1950. After a thorough evaluation, the USN placed an order for 29 training helicopters designated HTK-1. In 1962, this was changed to T-43E under the Department of Defense Joint Designation System.

RIGHT: **A HOK-1 in service with the US Marine Corps. For operations over South Vietnam, many were painted in jungle-type camouflage.**

While the T-43E was in production, Kaman developed the larger K-600, which was ordered for the US Marine Corps and US Navy as the HOK-1 and HUK-1 (for ship-support) respectively. In 1962, both were redesignated as UH-43C and OH-43D. The distinctively shaped helicopter had a boom-mounted tailplane fitted with three vertical fins for directional control.

ABOVE: **Although the Kaman H-43 Huskie was fitted with an unusual twin rotor system, the type had conventional collective and cyclic flight controls.**

The US Air Force also took delivery of the H-43A (later HH-43A) and named the type Huskie. Deliveries to the USAF began in November 1958. The H-43A was fitted with four vertical tail fins for improved directional control.

In 1951, Kaman had trialed the installation of a small Boeing YT-50 gas turbine engine in one of the development K-225 aircraft, thereby creating the first jet-powered helicopter. With this experience and research, Kaman began to experiment with the installation of a turboshaft engine in a HOK-1 airframe, and flight testing demonstrated significantly improved performance. As a result, the H-43B (later the HH-43B) was developed, and first flew on December 13, 1958.

Powered by an Avco Lycoming T53-L-1B turboshaft mounted on top of the airframe, the B model was larger and had accommodation for up to eight passengers. The significant improvements in performance made this version ideal for the search and rescue role.

A total of 193 were manufactured for the USAF, and this made the H-43B the most numerous variant of all. The USAF used the type primarily for the airfield crash and fire rescue role, and each machine carried a large tank containing 309 litres/63 gallons of chemical foam, a rescue crew wearing firefighting suits, and other special equipment.

The aircraft was fitted with a winch with a lifting capacity of 272kg/600lb. On alert, the crew of an H-43B could be airborne within 60 seconds and were often first in attendance at the scene of a crash. Downwash from the rotors could be used to great effect to deflect flames away from the crashed aircraft.

The H-43 was also exported to a number of foreign air arms under the US Military Assistance Program (MAP), including Burma, Pakistan, Colombia, Morocco and Thailand.

The H-43F was the final production variant. The aircraft was fitted with a more powerful engine and a larger fuselage to accommodate up to 11 passengers, and a total of 40 were supplied to the USAF. A further 17 of the type were built for Iran, and all were specially configured to operate in hot and high conditions.

The H-43F was used in South-east Asia on missions to rescue downed aircrew. The type was especially suited to jungle operations due to the crew being able to fly the aircraft into small clearings. It was also used to resupply US Navy gunboats (part of the so-called

ABOVE: **A Kaman HH-43B equipped with skids mounted on the undercarriage, allowing the machine to land on soft ground or snow.**

"Brown Water Navy") on patrol in the Mekong Delta. On these operations, the aircraft was particularly vulnerable to ground fire from Viet Cong forces, so a machine-gun could be mounted in the door opening for defence.

The H-43 Huskie was flown on more rescue missions during the Vietnam War than any other type of helicopter. In the early 1970s, the H-43 was gradually replaced in US military service by newer types of helicopter.

Kaman H-43B Huskie

First flight: September 27, 1956
Power: 1 x Lycoming 825 T53-L-1B turboshaft
Armament: None
Size: Rotor diameter – 14.43m/47ft
    Length – 26.9m/86ft 3in
    Height – 7.8m/25ft 7in
Weights: Empty – 2,027kg/4,469lb
    Take-off – 3,992kg/8,800lb (maximum)
Performance: Speed – 193kph/120mph (maximum)
    Service ceiling – 7,625m/25,000ft
    Range – 378km/235 miles

Kaman SH-2 Seasprite

After the considerable success of the earlier H-43 Huskie helicopter, it was a surprise that intermeshing rotor configuration was not used on the company's response to a 1956 US Navy requirement for a long-range search and rescue helicopter.

This helicopter, first flown on July 2, 1959, originally entered USN service as the Kaman HU2K-1. The single-engine helicopter was primarily deployed on USN aircraft carriers in the search and rescue role. In 1962, the type was redesignated UH-2A by the Department of Defense (DoD). By the end of 1965, a total of 190 utility and rescue UH-2A/B versions had been delivered. During the late 1960s, an upgrade programme was initiated, the major part of which was converting the aircraft to a twin-engine

configuration. The engines were linked to an uprated gearbox and transmission driving a four-blade rotor, which allowed a substantial increase load-carrying capacity.

The UH-2 Seasprite was ultimately developed as a shipborne combat helicopter with anti-submarine and anti-surface attack capability. In the late 1960s, Light Airborne Multi-Purpose System (LAMPS) was fitted to improve the type's operational capabilities. In operation, a LAMPS-equipped Seasprite was deployed to extend the defensive area around a warship and attack any submarine threat with torpedoes. In the defence role, LAMPS provided early warning of anti-shipping missile attack. LAMPS-equipped Seasprites were designated SH-2D and carried search radar, an Electronic Surveillance Measures (ESM) receiver, an active sonar repeater and a UHF acoustic data-relay transmitter. The type was

LEFT: A US Navy UH-2C Seasprite of helicopter Combat Support Squadron HC-1 Det. 19 aboard the aircraft carrier USS *Hancock* (CVA-19) on a deployment to Vietnam between July 1968 and March 1969.

ABOVE: A US Navy Kaman SH-2F Seasprite from Helicopter Light Anti-Submarine Squadron 30 (HSL-30) preparing to land on the destroyer USS *Nicholson* (DD-982).

also used for MEDEVAC, SAR, troop transport and supply missions.

The SH-2F was fitted with more powerful engines, an improved rotor, upgraded avionics and was equipped to tow a Magnetic Anomaly Detector (MAD). The tail wheel was moved forward to allow for operations from the decks of smaller ships. After a 16-year gap, the SH-2F was ordered back into production, an extremely rare occurrence in aviation history. From 1982, Kaman manufactured 54 new machines for the US Navy.

In 1987–88, the US Navy deployed the type on Operation Earnest Will (to protect Kuwaiti-owned oil tankers from attack by Iranian forces), the largest naval convoy operation since World War II. The type was used again in 1988 on Operation Praying Mantis (the attack by US naval forces in retaliation for the Iranian mining of a US warship). In 1991, the type was used operationally for the last time on

Operation Desert Storm (the invasion of Iraq). In October 1993, the SH-2F was retired from active USN service. At the time of retirement, the type was reported to require 30 maintenance hours for each hour flown, the highest rate for any aircraft in the US Navy inventory at that time.

Many machines were remanufactured as the SH-2G Super Seasprite, equipped with a much improved electronic warfare capability, and also

ABOVE: **An SH-2G Super Seasprite equipped with the Light Airborne Multi-Purpose System (LAMPS) operated by US Navy Reserve Helicopter Anti-Submarine Squadron (Light) 84, (HSL-84).**

more powerful engines that gave the type the highest power-to-weight ratio of any naval helicopter. The SH-2G entered the US Navy Reserve (USNR) inventory in February 1993, and was retired in May 2001. Currently, the SH-2G remains in military service with Egypt, Poland and New Zealand.

ABOVE: **Crew members aboard the battleship USS *Iowa* (BB-61) waiting for a Kaman SH-2F Seasprite to be secured before transporting an injured sailor during NATO exercise North Wedding 86.**

Kaman Seasprite

First flight: July 2, 1959

Power: 2 x General Electric T700-GE-401 turboshaft

Armament: Torpedoes, depth charges, anti-ship or anti–tank missiles, air-to-ground missiles, unguided rockets

Size: Rotor diameter – 13.5m/44ft
Length – 16m/52ft 6in
Height – 4.62m/15ft

Weights: Empty – 3,447kg/7,600lb
Take-off – 6,124kg/13,500lb (maximum)

Performance: Speed – 256kph/159mph (maximum)
Service ceiling – 6,218m/20,400ft
Range – 1,000km/620 miles

Kamov Ka-25

The Ka-25 (NATO codename Hormone) was developed to meet the specification for a Soviet Navy requirement of 1958 for an anti-submarine warfare helicopter that could be operated from the range of vessels in service with the Soviet Navy. In response, Kamov developed the Ka-20 (NATO identifier Harp) from the earlier Ka-15 design. In July 1961, the Ka-20 was first seen in public when it was flown at the Tushino Aviation Day carrying two dummy air-to-surface missiles. The Ka-20 immediately attracted the interest of Western military observers attending the display. Having proven the basic configuration, the type became the prototype for the production Ka-25.

ABOVE: **Two Kamov Ka-25PLs about to land on a Moskva-class cruiser of the Soviet Navy.**

The use of counter-rotating coaxial main rotor alleviates the requirement for an anti-torque tail rotor to be fitted. This allows the fuselage to have a very short tail boom, which saves much-needed deck storage space. The two three-bladed rotors also fold, to save space. The Ka-25 was powered by two Glushenkov GTD-3F turboshaft engines installed side by side above the cabin. In an emergency, the machine could be safely flown on one engine. The three vertical tail fins were fitted to provide directional stability.

A powerful search radar scanner, mounted in a housing under the nose, can detect a surface target as small as the periscope on a submarine. This radar is augmented by Magnetic Anomaly Detector (MAD) sensors,

LEFT: **The Kamov Ka-25T was equipped with a search radar and missiles for the anti-shipping attack role.**

LEFT: **The Kamov Ka-25PL was specifically equipped for anti-submarine warfare, and was operated from Kiev-class cruisers of the Soviet Navy.**

electro-optical sensors and dipping sonar which is lowered into the sea while the helicopter is flown at the hover. Although usually flown unarmed, production aircraft were fitted with an internal weapons bay to carry torpedoes or depth charges (including nuclear type) for anti-submarine attack.

Up to 25 variants of the type are thought to have been built, and among the numerous variations were the Ka-25B/Ka-25PL for anti-submarine warfare and the Ka-25T used for over-the-horizon guidance and targeting of ship-launched missiles. The Ka-25PS was developed as a search and rescue helicopter, and is equipped with a 300kg/660lb capacity winch, sensors to detect a pilot's distress beacon and a powerful searchlight for night operations.

Between 1966 and 1975, some 460 were produced to replace the Mil Mi-4 (NATO identifier Hound) as the primary ASW helicopter in Soviet Navy service. Ka-25s fitted with long-range variable depth sonar to detect enemy submarines were first deployed on board Moskva-class cruisers. The Soviet Navy

ABOVE: **A Kamov Ka-25PL fitted with undercarriage units for flight deck operations on ships of the Soviet Navy. Note the radar scanner housing under the nose.**

received four Kiev-class aircraft carriers which operated Ka-25s in the ASW role.

As well as the Soviet Navy and Russian Federation, the Ka-25 was used by Bulgaria, India, Syria, Ukraine, Vietnam and the former Yugoslavia.

Kamov Ka-25

First flight: 1961
Power: 2 x Glushenkov GTD-3F turboshaft
Armament: Torpedoes, depth charges
Size: Rotor diameter – 15.75m/51ft 8in
Length – 9.75m/32ft
Height – 5.4m/17ft 8in
Weights: Empty – 4,765kg/10,488lb
Take-off – 7,200kg/15,847lb (maximum)
Performance: Speed – 220kph/136mph (maximum)
Ceiling – 3,500m/11,483ft
Range – 400km/248 miles

Kamov Ka-27/Ka-29/Ka-31/Ka-32

Kamov began work on a successor to the Ka-25 in 1967, following requests from the Soviet Navy for a helicopter capable of operating night or day and in all weathers. Although broadly based on the Ka-25, the Ka-27 (NATO identifier Helix) was an all-new helicopter with dimensions similar to the Ka-25, and retaining the distinctive Kamov counter-rotating coaxial main rotor system.

The Ka-27 was flown for the first time in 1973, and remains in Russian Navy service as the standard Anti-Submarine Warfare (ASW) helicopter.

The Ka-27 is fitted with two vertical tail fins mounted on the tailplane at the end of the short tail boom. The type is powered by two Isotov TV3-117V turboshaft engines (well proven in Mil helicopters), which produce twice

ABOVE: **A Kamov Ka-27 (NATO identifier Helix) from the Russian destroyer *Admiral Vinogradov* flying near the guided-missile cruiser USS *Vella Gulf* (CG-72) while on operations in the Gulf of Aden.**

the power of those used in the Ka-25. A new type of advanced high-efficiency composite rotor blades and more engine power allows the Ka-27 to lift a payload that is 50 per cent heavier than the earlier design.

The production Ka-27PL ASW version which entered service in 1982 is fitted with a search radar scanner, dipping sonar and sonobouys. An enlarged weapons bay for up to four torpedoes is built into the underside of the fuselage. In action the aircraft is operated in pairs, with one tracking the enemy while the following helicopter launches the attack. Operating in this way, and in all weather conditions, the equipment can be used to detect, track

LEFT: **The coaxial rotor assembly and short tail boom are key recognition features of this series of helicopters.**

LEFT: **Although the Ka-27 was an all-new design, it was built to dimensions that were similar to the earlier Ka-25.**

military and has been in service since 1985. The type can be used as part of an amphibious assault force to transport troops and cargo. Although specialist transport or combat equipment is usually fitted on the production line, the type is versatile enough to be modified in the field if required. The fuselage can accommodate 16 fully equipped troops or four stretcher cases plus seven seated casualties. Cargo capacity is an impressive 2,032kg/4,480lb. For offensive operations, the armour-protected helicopter can be fitted with four hardpoints to carry rockets, bombs or machine-gun pods. Other loads can be carried in the torpedo bay. The helicopter is also fitted with a 7.62mm machine-gun. In 2001, the Ka-29 was used extensively by Russian forces on operations against Chechen rebels.

A further variant, the Ka-31, was developed for airborne early warning operations, and has a large foldable radar scanner mounted under the fuselage. The only export customer for this version was the Indian Navy.

A 16-passenger civil version, the Ka-32, was built, and some in Aeroflot markings have been seen operating from ships of the Russian Navy. This version is also equipped with a hook under the fuselage for lifting loads. More than 40 of the type are in service in North Korea. In July 2004, that country's air force took delivery of their first Ka-32 to be used for SAR operations.

and destroy a target at a submerged depth of 500m/1,641ft and running at speeds of up to 75kph/47mph.

The production version of the Ka-27PL also has a lengthened cockpit with additional windows. The lower section of the fuselage is watertight to allow an emergency landing on water. The Ka-27PL has a crew of three, a pilot, a tactical coordinator and an ASW systems operator.

A search and rescue (SAR) version of the Ka-27PS was developed, and on this machine the position for the ASW

weapons operator is used by the winchman when operating the 300kg/660lb capacity rescue winch.

Military operators of the Ka-27 include South Korea, Ukraine and Vietnam. A simpler version, the Ka-28 with revised avionics equipment, was exported to China and India. China purchased both the Ka-27 and Ka-28 to be operated from four Russian-built Sovremenny-class destroyers.

A multi-mission naval combat version, the Ka-29, has a wider front fuselage. It was also produced for the Russian

ABOVE: **A Kamov Ka-28 flying over the city of Niz, Serbia, equipped for firefighting – just one of the many roles that can be carried out by this versatile type of helicopter.**

Kamov Ka-27PL

First flight: 1973
Power: 2 x Klimov TV3-117V turboshaft
Armament: Torpedoes, depth charges
Size: Rotor diameter – 15.90m/52ft 2in
Length – 12.25m/40ft 2in
Height – 5.4m/17ft 8in
Weights: Empty – 6,100kg/13,338lb
Take-off – 12,600kg/27,778lb (maximum)
Performance: Speed – 250kph/155mph (maximum)
Ceiling – 5,004m/16,405ft
Range – 800km/496 miles

Kamov Ka-50/Ka-52

The Ka-50 (NATO identifier Hokum), was developed in the 1980s from the Kamov V-80Sh-1 prototype and was first seen in public at the Zhukovsky Air Show, near Moscow, in August 1992. The following month, the second production machine was displayed in the UK at the Farnborough Air Show. In November 1993, four production machines were delivered for trials with the Russian Army. In the late 1980s, large orders for the Ka-50 had appeared to be imminent, but the collapse of the Soviet Union in 1991 threw defence procurement into chaos. Only 12 of the type were delivered to the Russian Army in August 1995, not the expected hundreds. Production of the KA-50 was restarted in 2006, but only to complete five machines that were not delivered during the Soviet era.

Soviet military experience in Afghanistan showed that although the Mil Mi-24 was an excellent attack helicopter, it was found to be too large and lacked manoeuvrability. Also during

ABOVE: **The two-seat Kamov Ka-52 Alligator (NATO identifier Hokum-B) was designed to be the lead aircraft guiding a battle formation of Kamov Ka-50 Black Shark helicopters to the target.**

hazardous low-level operations, the type was found to be vulnerable to ground fire. A specification was issued by the military detailing a requirement for a compact, well-armed and manoeuvrable helicopter with an airframe that could absorb a lot of battle damage. The Ka-50, named Black Shark by the manufacturer, has an aircraft-type fuselage with a vertical tailfin, and is extremely manoeuvrable. The type is cleared to be aerobatic.

The lack of a tail rotor also greatly improves combat survivability. During the war in Afghanistan, many helicopter crews found that any damage to the tail boom or tail rotor could be catastrophic. The main gearbox is also safely mounted between the engines and is well protected.

LEFT: **The Kamov Ka-50 Black Shark (NATO identifier Hokum) can carry an impressive array of weapons, including 30mm cannon pods, unguided ground-attack rockets and anti-tank missiles.**

LEFT: **The Kamov Ka-50 Black Shark was the first production helicopter fitted with an ejection seat. Explosive charges detach the rotor blades before the rocket-powered seat is fired.**

The cockpit is protected by 55mm/2.1in bullet-proof glass and armour plating strong enough to sustain hits from 20mm ammunition.

The Ka-50 was the first production helicopter to be fitted with an ejection seat. The rotor blades are blown off by explosive charges before the NPP Zvezda K-37-800 rocket-powered seat is fired.

The helicopter is relatively light and consequently has an excellent power-to-weight ratio, allowing an impressive amount of weaponry to be carried on the two stub wings. Each wing has two hardpoints and a mounting on on each wingtip to carry rockets, missiles or gun pods. A heat suppressor mounted over each engine exhaust duct is designed to reduce the aircraft's infra-red signature, reducing the possibility of a strike by a heat-seeking missile. The Ka-50 can be flown on one engine in the event of battle damage.

In January 2001, the Ka-50 was first used in combat in an attack on Chechen positions, operated within a force of Ka-29 and Mi-24 attack helicopters.

The Ka-52 (NATO identifier Hokum-B), a two-seat development, was first flown in June 1997, and retains some 85 per cent of the original Ka-50 airframe. The type is intended to be deployed on the battlefront as the lead aircraft to a force of Ka-50s. The type is known as the Alligator, and is thought to be in limited service with the Russian special forces.

At the time of writing, the Russian Air Force were estimated to be operating 25 in a combined fleet of Ka-50 and Ka-52 helicopters.

ABOVE: **The Kamov Ka-50 Black Shark and the Ka-52 Alligator are at present only in service with the Russian Air Force, and it is estimated that a combined fleet of 25 are operational.**

Kamov Ka-50

First flight: July 27, 1982

Power: 2 x Klimov TV3-117VMA turboshaft

Armament: 30mm cannon AA-8 Aphid, AA-11 AAM, Archer, AT-9 Ataka or AT-16 Vikhr anti-tank, AS-10 Karen anti-radiation, AS-12 Kegler air-to-surface

Size: Rotor diameter – 14.5m/47ft 7in
Length – 16m/52ft 6in
Height – 4.93m/16ft 2in

Weights: Empty – 9,800kg/21,605lb
Take-off – 10,800kg/23,810lb (maximum)

Performance: Speed – 310kph/193mph (maximum)
Ceiling – 5,500m/18,030ft
Range – 460km/286 miles

MBB/Eurocopter Bo105

The Bo105 is light, two-engine, multi-purpose utility helicopter originally designed and developed by Bölkow in Germany. The type was manufactured by Messerschmitt-Bölkow-Blohm (MBB) until 1991, when the company became a part of Eurocopter.

Production of the Bo105 continued until 2001, by which time over 1,500 military and civil versions had been produced. The type is fitted with an advanced rigid-rotor system (designed in association with Aérospatiale) and two turboshaft engines, allowing the Bo105 to be highly manoeuvrable and fully aerobatic. The cockpit is designed to allow the crew excellent visibility through large unobstructed windows. The Bo105 is equipped for all-weather operation.

Design of the type began in 1962 and the prototype, powered by two Allison turboshaft engines, was first flown on February 16, 1967, with MBB test pilot Wilfried von Engelhardt at the controls. Civil certification was granted in 1970, and the machine entered production for German civil and law enforcement services, as well as for overseas customers.

RIGHT: **A Bo105E-4 in service with the Albanian Air Force, one of the many nations who ordered the type.**

The Bo105C version was developed during 1972, and the Ministry of Defence in West Germany ultimately chose the type for the light observation military helicopter programme and ordered 100 machines in 1977.

The German Army also procured 212 of the Bo105 PAH-1, an anti-tank version armed with six HOT missiles, a second-generation, long-range anti-tank missile system.

ABOVE: **A Bo105 PAH-1 equipped with HOT missiles of the German Army Aviators School from Heeresflugplatz Celle (Celle Air Base).**

An infra-red sight for the missile system, mounted on top of the cockpit directly above the pilot, allows the crew to observe potential targets at night and in all weathers, while the helicopter is held at the hover behind covering terrain.

ABOVE: **A salvo of 2.75in rockets being fired from a Bo105 of the Mexican Navy at the ex-USS *Connolly* (DE-306) target ship during the multi-national naval exercise Unitas Gold.**
RIGHT: **A Bo105 from Multi-Purpose Helicopter Squadron 40 (MH-40) being held at the hover prior to landing on USS *Essex* (LHD-2).**

The German Army Aviation Corps (Heeresfliegertruppe) was the largest operator of the type, with a total of over 300 in service. The type was also used in the battlefield observation and transport role. Bulky cargo was carried by a hook mounted under the fuselage. The load could be jettisoned instantly by operating an emergency release in the cockpit.

Other operators have included the Albanian Air Force, Chilean Air Force and Navy, Colombian Navy, Indonesian Air Force and Navy, Iraqi Air Force, Mexican Navy, Royal Netherlands Air Force, Philippine Air Force and Navy, Republic of Korea Army, Spanish Army, Swedish Air Force and Army and the Uruguayan Navy. Many overseas customers have deployed the Bo105 in the maritime patrol role. For the CASEVAC/MEDEVAC role, the helicopter can be fitted to carry two stretchers mounted behind the crew. Clamshell doors at the rear of the fuselage give access to the cargo compartment.

The civil version of the Bo105 has been used for many duties, including emergency rescue, law enforcement, ambulance, SAR (fitted with infra-red sensors and a powerful searchlight) and mountain rescue.

MBB Bo105

First flight: February 16, 1967
Power: 2 x Allison 250-C20B turboshaft
Armament: HOT anti-tank missiles
Size: Rotor diameter – 9.84m/32ft 4in
    Length – 11.86m/38ft 11in
    Height – 3m/9ft 10in
Weights: Empty – 1,280kg/2,820lb
    Take-off – 2,400kg/5,290lb (maximum)
Performance: Speed – 242kph/150mph (maximum)
    Service ceiling – 5,185m/17,000ft
    Range – 585km/363 miles

Mil Mi-1

Designed by Mikhail Mil, the Mi-1 was the first Soviet helicopter to go into series production, and the first helicopter to enter service with the Soviet military. During World War II, Mil led the Soviet experimental helicopter section, having had pre-war experience working with Nikolai Ilyich Kamov, a pioneer in Soviet helicopter development. The prototype, designated GM-1 (Gelikopter Mil), was built and flown in 1948 with test pilot M. K. Baikalov at the controls. The machine was fitted with a single main rotor, a fully enclosed cockpit (for a pilot and up to three passengers) and an all-metal monocoque-type fuselage. Baikalov was later killed in one of the prototypes when it crashed due to the failure of a weld in the tail-rotor bearing assembly. The aircraft was powered by a single Ivchenko AI-26V radial petrol engine.

The rotor blades were constructed from steel and plywood with fabric covering. An anti-torque rotor with wooden blades was fitted at the rear of the tail boom. A long skid was fitted under the end of the tail boom to protect the tail rotor from damage during take-off and landing. The underside of the nose was glazed to give the pilot the best possible view on landing. Production versions were equipped with a radio altimeter, the aerial for which was mounted under the tail boom. Fuel in all versions was carried in a 240-litre/53-gallon aluminium tank. To allow an increase in range, a 160-litre/35-gallon auxiliary fuel tank could be carried externally on the starboard side of the fuselage.

The type was already in Soviet military service when eight were displayed in public for the first time at the 1951 Tushino Aviation Day. Production of the Mi-1 (NATO identifier Hare) took place over a 16-year period

ABOVE: **This Mil Mi-1M, once operated by the Hungarian Air Force, is fitted with enclosed stretcher-carrying panniers. The machine is displayed at the Museum of Hungarian Aviation, Szolnok.**

ABOVE AND RIGHT: The Mil Mi-1 was widely used in many Warsaw Pact countries, including Poland. A total of some 1,500 were manufactured in Poland as the SM-1.

in the Soviet Union, where some 1,000 were built. Production of the type, designated SM-1, by WSK PZL at Swidnik in Poland began in 1955, and over 1,500 airframes were completed. Aviation commentators at the time observed the similarities between the Mi-1 and the US-built Sikorsky S-51, as well as the British-built Bristol Type 171 Sycamore. The type was widely exported to be used by the military air arms of other Warsaw Pact countries and other Soviet-friendly nations. The Mil Mi-1 was used in a variety of roles, including reconnaissance, transport, SAR, MEDEVAC (fitted with external temperature-controlled stretcher panniers mounted on the sides of the fuselage), training and observation. Float-equipped versions were also produced.

This was a period of development and innovation in helicopter technology so as production of the type continued, it was improved and refined, leading to a major improvement in reliability. In keeping with most Soviet equipment, the helicopter was designed to operate in cold, harsh conditions, being fitted with de-icing systems for both the rotor and cockpit windscreen.

Overseas military operators included the Afghan Air Force, Albanian Air Force, Algerian Air Force, People's Republic of China, Cuban Air Force, Czechoslovak Air Force, East German Air Force, Egyptian Air Force, Finnish Air Force, Hungarian Air Force, Iraqi Air Force, Mongolian People's Air Force, North Korean Air Force, Romanian Air Force and Syrian Air Force.

ABOVE: The Mi-1 had a fixed nosewheel landing gear equipped with brakes. The machine is fitted with an auxillary fuel tank on the side of the fuselage to provide an increase in range.

Mil Mi-1

First flight: September 20, 1948
Power: 1 x Ivchenko AI-26V piston engine
Armament: None
Size: Rotor diameter – 14.35m/47ft 1in
    Length – 12.09m/39ft 8in
    Height – 3.30m/10ft 10in
Weights: Empty – 1,700kg/3,740lb
    Take-off – 2,330kg/5,126lb (maximum)
Performance: Speed – 205kph/127mph (maximum)
    Ceiling – 3,500m/11,480ft
    Range – 590km/367 miles

LEFT: **The Mil Mi-2 (NATO identifier Hoplite) was based on the airframe of the earlier Mi-1. The machine was fitted with two turboshaft engines driving a single gearbox installation positioned above the cabin.**

Mil Mi-2

Just a few years after the first true helicopter designs were in service, it was clear that the turboshaft engine gave designers the ability to build bigger, more efficient helicopters. The Mi-2 (NATO identifier Hoplite) was based on the Mi-1, but was fitted with an all-new two-turboshaft engine and gearbox installation (designed by Isotov) positioned on top of the helicopter, driving a three-blade main rotor and a two-blade tail rotor. This arrangement allowed much more cabin space. The new powerplant installation also made the helicopter less affected by changes to the Centre of Gravity (CoG)

from cabin cargo or passengers. The aircraft was fitted with a nose-wheel-type tricycle undercarriage.

With more power and lighter engines, the Mi-2 offered a significantly improved weight-carrying capability compared to the earlier machine, and the type was soon being developed for a range of both military and civilian roles. The Mi-2 became the Bell UH-1 of the Soviet Union.

The V2 prototypes had been flown in Russia but all production of the Mi-2 was undertaken by PZL-Swidnik, near Lublin in Poland. The first Polish-built machine flew on November 4, 1965. Over the

following 26-year manufacturing period, a total of 5,080 machines were produced, mainly for military use.

The type was widely exported outside the Soviet Union. Military operators included Afghanistan, Albania, Algeria, Armenia, Azerbaijan, Belarus, Bulgaria, China, Cuba, East Germany, Hungary, Czechoslovakia and Poland. Many were transferred to other states, including Djibouti, Estonia, Ethiopia, Cambodia, Georgia, Ghana, Indonesia, India, Iraq, Latvia and Liberia. The type was also delivered to Lesotho, Libya, Lithuania, Mongolia, Mexico, Myanmar, Nicaragua, North Korea, Peru, Syria and Turkey.

LEFT: **The main rotor blades on the Mi-2 are constructed from a metal spar and ribs covered with aluminium. The main and tail rotors are fitted with an electrically heated de-icing system, essential for the harsh weather conditions of the Soviet Union.**

PZL developed 25 versions for both military and civilian use from firefighting to training, ambulance (with four stretchers mounted side-by-side), SAR, photographic survey and reconnaissance.

The Mi-2URN Zimija (viper) was a gunship version armed with two pods, each containing 16 unguided rockets, a fixed 23mm NS-23 cannon on the starboard side of the fuselage, plus a cabin-mounted machine-gun to be fired by a crew member. The later Mi-2US was armed with two pod-mounted 7.62mm PKT machine-guns, as well as a fixed 23mm NS-23 cannon and a cabin-mounted machine-gun. The Mi-2URP Salamandra (salamander) was an anti-tank version armed with four AT-3 Sagger (9M14M Malyutka) wire-guided guided missiles with four "reload" missiles carried in the cabin. The Mi-2 URP-G Gniewosz carried four Strela 2 air-to-air missiles (AAM) for missions as an escort helicopter. In this dangerous role, the Mi-2URP-G was equipped with a radar warning receiver system to alert the pilot to any threat from enemy radar.

Many Mi-2s remain in front-line military service around the world. In the USA, a Cold War museum is reported to have operated four of the type on air-experience flights for their visitors. The US Army also operated the Mi-2 as part of a training programme for pilots to learn the flight characteristics of Soviet-era helicopter types.

ABOVE: **The Mil-2 can carry 700kg/1,545lb in the cabin, or 800kg/1,765lb in a cargo net suspended from a hook mounted on the underside of the fuselage.**

Mil Mi-2

First flight: November 4, 1965
Power: 2 x Isotov GTD-350P turboshaft
Armament: None
Size: Rotor diameter – 14.56m/47ft 9in
Length – 11.94m/39ft 2in
Height – 3.75m/12ft 4in
Weights: Empty – 2,402kg/5,485lb
Take-off – 3,700kg/8,140lb (maximum)
Performance: Speed – 210kph/130mph (maximum)
Service ceiling – 4,000m/13,125ft
Range – 170km/105 miles

Mil Mi-4

In 1951, Stalin had demanded a "sudden, great advance in Soviet helicopters", having noted the successful use of helicopters during the Korean War. The Mil design team may well have examined a Sikorsky S-55 as a source of inspiration but produced a machine that, although similar in appearance, was larger and had a better lift capacity. The Mil Mi-4 (NATO codename Hound) was developed in an impressively short time and was first flown by May 1952. The type was first displayed to the public at the 1953 Tushino Aviation Day in Moscow. By 1954, the Mi-4 was in military service, thus providing the Soviet leader with the advance in helicopter technology he had demanded.

The layout of the Mi-4 was, like the S-55, designed with ease of maintenance in mind. The engine, a proven Shvetsov Ash-82V radial piston engine (developed from the US-built Wright Cyclone), was installed at an angle in the nose behind large doors for easy access. The four-blade rotor was driven from the gearbox through a drive shaft that passed between the crew seats to the rotor hub. Unlike the Sikorsky S-55, the Mil Mi-4 had clamshell rear doors that not only made loading of freight much simpler, but were removable to enable infantry (up to 14 fully equipped troops could be carried) to exit rapidly during an airborne assault. In place of troops,

up to 1,600kg/3,530lb of cargo could be carried in the cabin, and often included small vehicles or light artillery.

At first, serious problems with the rotor kept the Mi-4 out of service. The wood-skinned and Bakelite (an early plastic) blades had a very short life of 100 hours before having to be replaced. In 1954, design and material improvements had allowed this time period to be increased to 300 hours, and by 1957 to 600 hours. By 1960, when all-metal rotor blades were fitted, this was increased to 1,500 hours.

The basic version of the Mi-4 was the 12–14 passenger military transport. Among the numerous variants produced was the Mi-4PLO, an anti-submarine warfare version fitted with a radome under the nose, a ventral observer station, dipping sonar, depth charges, sonobuoys and Magnetic Anomaly Detection (MAD) equipment. The Mi-4A was a military assault version with a ventral gun position on the underside of the fuselage fitted with a 12.7mm machine-gun with 200 rounds of ammunition. The Mi-4KP was an airborne command post, and the Mi-4M was an attack version armed with a chin gun turret in the nose and external rocket pods.

The Mi-4 was widely used by the Soviet armed forces (army, air force and navy), as well as by Warsaw Pact or Soviet-friendly nations. Albania, which phased out the type in 2005, is believed to have been the last military user of the Mi-4. Other operators were the Afghan Air Force, Algerian Air Force, Angola People's Air Defence Force, Bangladesh Air Force, Bulgarian Air Force and Navy, Burkina Faso, Cambodian Air Force, Cameroon

LEFT: The Mi-4M was one of few helicopters ever to be equipped with a gun turret as well as rocket pods.

Air Force, People's Republic of China and the Fuerza Aérea Revolucionaria in Cuba. Other military operators included the Egyptian Air Force, Finnish Air Force, Indian Air Force, Indonesian Air Force, Iraqi Air Force, Mongolian

People's Air Force and the North Korean Air Force. The type was also used by Sierra Leone, Somali Air Corps, South Yemen, Tajikistan, Syrian Air Force, Sudanese Air Force, Vietnam People's Air Force and the Yemen Air Force.

ABOVE: **The Mil Mi-4 was the first Soviet-built helicopter designed to be fitted with hydraulically boosted flight controls.**

When Soviet production ended in 1964, some 3,200 military and civil versions had been produced. From 1959 to 1965 in China, Harbin built a further 545 of the type under licence as the Z-5, powered by an HS7 radial piston engine. The prototype of the Z-5 was first flown on December 14, 1958.

BELOW: **Between 1959 and 1965, the Mi-4 was built by Harbin in the People's Republic of China as the Z-5. The machine was powered by a Chinese-built HS7 radial piston engine.**

Mil Mi-4

First flight: May, 1952
Power: 1 x Shvetsov ASh-82V piston engine
Armament: 12.7mm machine-gun
Size: Rotor diameter – 21.00m/68ft 11in
Length – 25.02m/82ft 1in
Height – 5.18m/17ft
Weights: Empty – 6,626kg/14,608lb
Take-off – 7,534kg/16,610lb (maximum)
Performance: Speed – 200kph/124mph (maximum)
Service ceiling – 5,486m/18,000ft
Range – 500km/313 miles

Mil Mi-6

The Mi-6 (NATO identifier Hook) was first flown in June 1957. For some time it was both the largest helicopter in the world and, with a speed of 300kph/186mph, the fastest. It was also the first turboshaft-powered helicopter to be designed and built in the Soviet Union. The enormous five-blade main rotor has a diameter of 35m/114ft 10in and the overall length of the machine with the rotor turning is 41.74m/137ft, larger than the wingspan of a Lockheed C-130 Hercules. Between 1957 and 1980, some 800 were built for military and civil operators.

Originally developed to meet a joint Soviet Air Force/Aeroflot requirement for a heavy-lift helicopter, the Mi-6 is a complex aircraft and has a flight crew of two pilots, a flight engineer, a navigator and a radio operator. The Soviet Union had remote, undeveloped areas without airfields that had to be accessed quickly for both military and commercial reasons. The Mi-6 had a specially developed rotor de-icing system for operations in sub-zero conditions. The tail rotor (larger than the main rotor of some helicopters) was fitted with electric heating in early versions, but this was

replaced with chemical de-icing in later versions. The main rotor blades had a steel main spar and were covered with aluminium. The tail rotor blades also had a steel spar but were covered with Bakelite plastic. The Mi-6 is powered by two Soloviev D-25V turboshaft engines driving the main rotor through a single gearbox which weighs 3,200kg/7,040lb.

The Mi-6 has a very large cabin for a helicopter and can carry up 70 fully equipped troops on seats fitted along the cabin sides and on a line of seats down the centre of the cabin. The type can be fitted for the MEDEVAC role to carry 41 stretchers and two medical attendants. The maximum internal payload is 12,000kg/26,450lb (more than a Sikorsky CH-54 Tarhe), and a cargo of 8,000kg/17,637lb can be carried slung under the helicopter. In October 1957, the type was used to set a new weight-to-height record by lifting 10,174kg/22,400lb to altitude. In 1961, on another record flight, this was increased to 20,117kg/44,800lb to a height of 2,745m/9,000ft.

LEFT: **The Mil Mi-10 flying crane was developed from the Mi-6, and entered service in 1963. It was built in both short-undercarriage (Mi-10K) and long-undercarriage (Mi-10R) versions.**

Large clamshell rear doors facilitate the loading of bulky cargo, including the PT-76 tracked carrier mounted with a FROG-7 battlefield missile, trucks or heavy artillery. The Mi-6 was designed to carry all types of armoured personnel carriers, armoured cars and light mechanized infantry vehicles in service with Soviet military forces.

Special versions included the Mi-6PS search and rescue helicopter developed in 1966 for the recovery of Vostok, Voshkod and Soyuz space vehicles. The Mi-6VKP was equipped as a command post and fitted with specialized electronic warfare

equipment – a T-shaped antennae is mounted on the tail boom.

In addition to service with the Soviet military, the Mi-6 was operated by a number of Warsaw Pact and Soviet-friendly nations, including Afghanistan, Algeria, Azerbaijan, Belarus, Bulgaria, People's Republic of China, Egypt, Ethiopia, Indonesia, Iraq, Kazakhstan, Lao People's Liberation Army Air Force, Peru, Poland, Syria, Ukraine, Uzbekistan, Vietnam and Zimbabwe.

Between 1979 and 1989, ten of the type were lost in accidents or to enemy fire during Soviet operations in Afghanistan.

ABOVE: **Troops exiting a Peruvian Air Force Mi-6 as another lands during an air-assault exercise.**

Mil Mi-6

First flight: June 5, 1957
Power: 2 x Soloviev D-25V turboshaft
Armament: 12.7mm machine-gun
Size: Rotor diameter – 35m/115ft
    Length – 41.74m/137ft
    Height – 9.86m/32ft
Weights: Empty – 27,240kg/59,928lb
    Take-off – 42,500kg/93,700lb (maximum)
Performance: Speed – 300kph/186mph (maximum)
    Service ceiling – 4,500m/14,750ft
    Range – 620km/384 miles

RIGHT: **The size of this Mi-6 can be appreciated as it dwarfs nearby cars. Note the large shoulder wings, which generate up to 20 per cent of the aerodynamic lift.**

LEFT: The main rotor blades on the Mil Mi-8 (NATO identifier Hip) are manufactured from an aluminium alloy and fitted with an electro-thermal de-icing system. The blades also have an internal gas pressurization system to aid the detection of cracks caused by metal fatigue.

Mil Mi-8

Powerful, easy to maintain and economical to operate, the Mi-8 (NATO identifier Hip) has been produced in greater numbers than almost any other helicopter, and has served in more than 50 air arms around the world. More than 11,000 have been built, including the Mi-17 variant (by comparison, Sikorsky built some 1,500 Sea Kings), and it has been operated in a variety of roles, from troop carrier, gunship, search and rescue to command post. When the type was first displayed in 1961, it was larger and appeared as powerful as any Western-built helicopter. The popular notion that the Soviet Union was somehow only capable of copying Western designs was laid to rest.

Intended to succeed the Mi-4, the V-8 prototype was a single-engine design that evolved into the Mi-8. However, both Aeroflot (the Soviet state airline) and the Soviet military required two engines for extra power and operational safety. Mil then designed and produced a twin-engine version of the V-8 with two turboshafts mounted (as on the Mi-6) above the cabin. The first test flight,

BELOW: Two Mil Mi-8 helicopters delivering Egyptian infantry during an air-assault exercise in desert conditions.

RIGHT: **Ease of maintenance and comparatively low operating costs made the Mi-8 an attractive buy for many export customers. Production of the Mi-8 was carried out by Mil plants at Kazan and Ulan-Ude.**

on September 17, 1962, was successful, and the design was refined and perfected until the Mi-8 was ready for production in 1965. The type entered Soviet Air Force service in 1967. Export orders followed soon after the Mi-8 was demonstrated at the 1965 Paris Air Show.

The Mi-8 has been built in a large number of military variants, the most numerous being the tactical assault helicopter which accounted for some 9,000 of the total production run. Other versions included utility, electronic warfare and border surveillance when equipped with special sensors. The gunship variant was armed with a nose mounted gun, unguided rockets and anti-tank missiles carried on external pylons. Other military versions have been produced for mine laying and clearance, CASEVAC, tactical reconnaissance, photographic duties and spacecraft recovery.

The Mi-8 has been deployed for combat in many very different environments at locations around the world. The troop transport version was

BELOW: **An Mi-17 of the Macedonian Air Force. The Mi-17 is the export version of the Mi-8MT.**

widely used to launch many infantry assaults by Soviet forces during the 1979–89 war in Afghanistan. Some 40 of the type were shot down by Taliban forces. The Mi-8 was extensively used by Russian forces in Chechnya.

The type has also been used in battle during the Indo–Pakistan war of the early 1970s. The Mil-8 was deployed during the Arab–Israeli war of 1973–74, where the Egyptian Air Force made extensive use of the type to land tactical assault troops, delivering stores and ammunition, and also SAR operations. The Mi-8 was used by Iraqi forces in the protracted Iran–Iraq war of 1980–88, and again during the Gulf War of 1991.

Between April and May 1986, a large number of Mi-8s were used to drop radiation-absorbing material on the reactor area at the devastated Chernobyl nuclear power plant. The majority of these helicopters were abandoned near the site after becoming contaminated with radioactive dust.

The Mi-17 is an improved version with uprated engines and can be identified by the tail rotor being positioned on the port side of the tail boom. An additional starboard door is fitted and the clamshell doors at the rear of the cargo hold replaced. The Mi-17 can carry up to 36 fully equipped troops able to exit the helicopter in three groups through the two side doors and a ramp at the rear.

Many civilian and military versions remain in service around the world. The enormous scale of production and the type's longevity of service must define the Mi-8 as one of the world's greatest helicopters.

Mil Mi-8

First flight: September 17, 1962
Power: 2 x Klimov (Isotov) TV-2-117A turboshaft
Armament: Rockets or anti-tank missiles
Size: 21.29m/69ft 11in each
    Length – 25.24m/82ft 9in
    Height – 5.65m/18ft 6in
Weights: Empty – 7,160kg/15,752lb
    Take-off – 12,000kg/26,400lb (maximum)
Performance: Speed – 250kph/155mph (maximum)
    Service ceiling – 4,500m/15,000ft
    Range – 500km/311 miles

Mil Mi-14

The Mi-14 (NATO identifier Haze) was developed from the successful Mi-8 as a dedicated naval helicopter for service within the Soviet Union, and was produced in anti-submarine, mine-countermeasures and search and rescue versions. The type was first flown in September 1969, and after a protracted development programme entered service in the mid-1970s as a replacement for the ageing Mi-4 helicopters. The Mi-14 was in

the main land-based, being too large to be stowed on the Kiev-class aircraft carriers then in service with the Soviet Navy.

One of the main differences between the Mi-14 and the Mi-8 was that the fuselage was designed with a boat-type hull for amphibious operations. Sponsons were fitted on the rear fuselage for stability on water. An additional small float was fitted on the underside of the tail boom

ABOVE: **More powerful engines were required to compensate for the extra weight of the amphibious hull and undercarriage retraction equipment.**

to keep the tail rotor clear of the water. The box-shaped item mounted on the underside of the tail boom is a Doppler navigation radar scanner.

The Mi-14PL is an anti-submarine warfare version and is equipped with a chin-mounted radar scanner, dipping

LEFT: **Normally, the Mi-14 has a crew of three, but the Mi-14PL has a crew of four – two pilots, a flight engineer and a systems operator.**

sonar and a towed APM-60 Magnetic Anomaly Detection (MAD) system to detect enemy submarine activity far below the ocean surface. When not in use, the MAD "sled" is stowed outside the rear of the main cabin.

A weapons bay in the hull carried OKA-2 sonobuoys to aid in the detection of submarines together with a retractable search radar. The Mi-14 was also armed with torpedoes and depth charges. A nuclear depth bomb, developed at the height of the Cold War, was part of the weapons inventory. The Mi-14PL can also be armed with air-to-surface missiles for use against surface vessels. In Polish service this type was designated Mi-14PW, and only the SAR version was available for

export. An improved ASW version was developed, the Mi-14PLM, with more powerful engines and improved detection equipment.

The Mi-14PS was the dedicated SAR version developed from the Mi-14PL but with an enlarged cabin door and a rescue hoist. A powerful searchlight was also fitted to enable rescues at night and in adverse weather conditions. The Mi-14PS carried ten 20-place life rafts. Ten survivors could be accommodated on board the helicopter and the empty life rafts towed behind the machine.

For mining operations the Mi-14BT was developed to tow a minesweeping sled to clear shipping channels of acoustic, magnetic and contact mines in preparation for an amphibious

landing. A seat for the tow operator was positioned in the rear fuselage. The winch was fitted to the rear of the fuselage mounted inside an aerodynamic fairing. This version of the Mi-14 could also be used to lay mines carried in the weapons bay.

By 1991, some 230 had been produced, and in addition to those supplied to the Soviet Air Force and Soviet Navy, many were exported to Warsaw Pact forces, including the Bulgarian Navy, East German Air Force, East German Navy, Polish Navy and the Yugoslav Air Force. The Mi-14 was also operated by the Cuban Navy, Ethiopian Air Force, Georgian Air Force, Libyan Air Force, North Korean Air Force, Syrian Naval Aviation, Ukrainian Naval Aviation and Yemen. Many of the type remain in service with these air arms or their successors.

ABOVE **The type has been produced in anti-submarine, search and rescue, firefighting, minesweeping and transport versions.**

Mil Mi-14PL

First flight: September, 1969
Power: 2 x Klimov (Isotov) TV3-117MT turboshaft
Armament: Torpedoes, bombs
Size: Rotor diameter – 21.29m/69ft 11in
  Length – 25.3m/83ft
  Height – 6.93m/22ft 9in
Weights: Empty – 8,900kg/19,625lb
  Take-off – 14,000kg/30,865lb (maximum)
Performance: Speed – 230kph/143mph (maximum)
  Service ceiling – 3,500m/11,500ft
  Range – 1,135km/704 miles

Mil Mi-24

The Mil Mi-24 (NATO identifier Hind) is a large helicopter designed for attack duties, such as anti-tank operations and close air support, but with accommodation to transport up to eight fully armed troops. Over 2,000 have been delivered over the past 40 years. In 2007, the Russian Air Force announced its intention to replace all Mi-24s in service with Mi-28 and Ka-50 attack helicopters. The Mi-24 is operated worldwide by around 50 nations and has given a number of nicknames by aircrew, such as "The Flying Tank", "Crocodile" (due to its style of camouflage) and "Glass" (after the distinctive double-bubble canopy over the tandem cockpit).

The Mi-24 entered service in 1969 with the closest comparative transport model at the time being the Bell UH-1A Iroquois, used for moving US troops to and from battlegrounds throughout the Vietnam War. During this period, the US military was investigating ways of improving individual helicopter types to advance efficiency in built-for-purpose roles (e.g. attack, gunship or transport). The Soviets were examining ways of

ABOVE: **There are at least 10 variants of the basic Mi-24, including the Mi-25 and Mi-35.**

BELOW: **Mil Mi-35 helicopters of the Afghan National Air Corps taking off in formation, to practise for the Afghan National Day in Kabul.**

combining roles within one type of helicopter. The Mi-24 was based on the same configuration as the Mi-8, two turboshaft engines positioned on top of the fuselage driving a five-blade main rotor and a three-blade tail rotor. The airframe is covered with anti-impact armour able to withstand hits from 0.50in ammunition. The rotor blades are constructed from titanium and can absorb hits from similar calibre ammunition. The cockpit canopies are moulded in armoured glass and are designed to resist 37mm cannon fire.

After significant combat experience during Soviet operations in Afghanistan between 1979 and 1989, the combined role of troop transport and gunship was finally discontinued due to the weight penalty. With less weight, the Mi-24 became more manoeuvrable and is commonly compared to the Sikorsky S-67 Black Hawk in service with US forces. The Mi-24 was designed to be fast – to reduce risk to on-board troops and to provide the adequate fire support to ground troops. To achieve this, the design team included a retractable tricycle landing undercarriage to reduce drag. The fuselage was streamlined and the stub wings also provided some lift at high speed. To create a more stable firing platform, the main rotor was tilted a few degrees to the right of the fuselage and the landing gear positioned to the left. The tail rotor was also asymmetrical to produce enough side force to compensate for the tilted main rotor.

The combat history of the Mi-24 is unparalleled by any other helicopter, Russian or otherwise. Since the 1970s, the type has been operated in over 26 separate conflicts, particularly in civil wars in the developing world (Sierra Leone, Cote d'Ivoire and Congo). The type was also seen on the battlefield during the Libyan civil crisis in 2011.

LEFT: **The Cyprus Air Command operates 11 examples of the Mi-35P, the export version of the Mi-24P.**

ABOVE: **Early versions of the Mil Mi-24 were armed with a Yakushev-Borzov 12.7mm YaK-B Gatling-type rotary machine-gun in a remote-controlled turret. The gun was linked to a sighting system mounted under the nose of the aircraft.**

Mil Mi-24

First flight: September 19, 1969
Power: 2 x Isotov TV3-117 turboshaft
Armament: 12.7mm machine-gun, 23mm cannon, rocket-launcher pod, cannon pod, grenade launcher, bomb, anti-tank missiles
Size: Rotor diameter – 17.3m/57ft
Length – 21.35m/70ft 1in
Height – 6.5m/21ft 3in
Weights: Empty – 8,500kg/18,740lb
Take-off – 12,000kg/26,500lb (maximum)
Performance: Speed – 335kph/208mph (maximum)
Service ceiling – 4,500m/14,750ft
Range – 750km/465 miles

LEFT: **Venezuela was among the large number of nations to procure the Mil Mi-26 (NATO identifier Halo) for military operations.**

Mil Mi-26

The Mil Mi-26 (NATO identifier Halo) is a true heavy-lift helicopter. In fact, it is the largest in the world, has twice the take-off weight of the Boeing CH-47 Chinook and an internal capacity similar in size to that of a Lockheed C-130 Hercules. This gigantic machine was first flown on December 17, 1977, and entered service with the Soviet military as a replacement for the Mil Mi-6 during 1983. The type remains operational, and over 300 have been built in both civil and military versions. The Mi-26 has been to exported to customers in more than 30 countries around the world.

In the early 1970s, a technical specification was issued for a helicopter with an empty weight (without fuel), which was not to be more than 50 per cent of the maximum take-off weight. The result was the Mil Mi-26, designed by Marat Tishchenko, a protégé of Mikhail Mil, the founder of the design bureau. The helicopter is powered by two Lotarev D-136 turboshaft engines mounted on top of the fuselage, which drive the unconventional eight-blade main rotor through a gearbox. The five-blade tail rotor is mounted on a fin at the end of the tail boom.

In 1982, the heavy-lift capability of the Mi-26 was demonstrated when a total mass of 56,768.8kg/124,948lb was raised to an altitude of 2,000m/ 6,562ft. The type is available in any of 16 different variants, including the Mi-26P, a civil air transport with accommodation for 63 passengers in airliner-type seating. The same variant was used as a military transport with a capacity for 65 fully equipped troops.

BELOW: **The Mil Mi-26 is fitted with a distinctive eight-blade main rotor system. The type has a five-blade tail rotor.**

The Mi-26MS is fitted out for the MEDEVAC role and can carry up to 65 stretchers and four/five attendants. An Anti-Submarine Warfare (ASW) version (Mi-26NEF-M) equipped with search radar and Magnetic Anomaly Detector (MAD) equipment is also in service. Other versions are the Mi-26TP for firefighting operations, the Mi-26PK/TM flying crane and the Mi-26TZ air-to-air refuelling tanker. Access to the interior of the machine is through three clamshell doors at the rear of the fuselage; two of them hinge outward while the third has an integral ramp for loading.

In 2002, after Operation Anaconda in Afghanistan, Lt Col Chuck Jarnot was instructed to organize the recovery of two US Army Chinook helicopters which had been shot down during the action and abandoned on a mountainside. With no heavy-lift capability available within the US military, Jarnot contacted a civilian operator of the Mi-26 based in Belgium. Six weeks later, the aircraft arrived in Afghanistan, flown by an East European crew. The operation was carried out using the under-fuselage cargo hook (lifting capacity 30,000kg/66,138lb) to recover the aircraft. The only Mi-26 in North America is a civilian version being operated for the oil industry in Canada.

The type has been used not only for recovery missions but, significantly, for the transport of heavy equipment to remote regions affected by disaster. In May 2008, an earthquake hit the Sichaun province in China, and Mil Mi-26 helicopters were used to airlift in earth-moving tractors to remove landslides which had blocked rivers causing severe flooding over vast areas, threatening the lives of the local population. Military operators of the type have included the Belarus Air Force, Royal Cambodian Air Force, Air Force of the Democratic Republic of the Congo, Indian Air Force, Kazakh Air Defence Forces, Mexican Air Force, Peruvian Army, Russian Air Force, Russian Army, Ukrainian Air Force, Ukraine Army and the Venezuelan Air Force.

LEFT: **One of two Mil Mi-26TC helicopters based in Greece and equipped for firefighting operations. A large volume of water or fire-retardant chemical is being carried under the machine in a purpose-designed hopper to be discharged over the fire.**

ABOVE: **Current operators of the Mil Mi-26 include the air forces of India, the Russian Federation and Ukraine. Aeroflot, the national airline of Russia, has also operated the type.**

Mil Mi-26

First flight: December 14, 1977
Power: 2 x Lotarev D-136 turboshaft
Armament: None
Size: Rotor diameter – 32m/105ft
Length – 40.025m/131ft 4in
Height – 8.15m/26ft 9in
Weights: Empty – 28,200kg/2,170lb
Take-off – 56,000kg/123,450lb (maximum)
Performance: Speed – 295kph/183mph (maximum)
Service ceiling – 4,600m/15,100ft
Range – 1,920km/1,190 miles

LEFT: **The Mil Mi-28 (NATO identifier Havoc) has a crew of two personnel seated in separate heavily armoured cockpits. The structure, including the windows, is manufactured to withstand direct hits from up to 12.7mm ammunition.**

Mil Mi-28

The Mil Mi-28 (NATO identifier Havoc) is a day or night all-weather attack helicopter. Whereas the Mil Mi-24 had a secondary troop transport capability, the Mi-28 is only designed for attack. Development of the type began in 1972, when both sides in the Cold War were trying to learn from operational experience in the Vietnam War in terms of the effectiveness of the helicopter in the attack role or as a gunship. The outline design was informed by the need to improve performance and speed on Soviet helicopters tasked with ground attack. The Mi-28 is often considered to be the Russian equivalent of the AH-64 Apache. The first of three Mi-28A prototypes was flown on November 10, 1982.

The Mi-28 has a conventional helicopter gunship cockpit layout with the crew sitting in tandem, the gunner in front of the pilot. A 30mm Shipunov 2A42 cannon in a barbette mounting is positioned under the nose of the aircraft. The wings on the machine each have two hardpoints

to carry a variety of weapons, including the Sheksna anti-tank missile, Ataka-V or S-8/13 unguided rocket, 23mm Gsh-23L gun pod, Igla-V or Vympel R-73 air-to-air missile and the KMGU-2 mine dispenser.

The Mi-28N (N – Night) version was launched and first flew on November 14, 1996. Described in the company's sales literature as a "round-the-clock operation combat helicopter", the type is equipped to locate and attack enemy armour and also low-speed air targets (including other helicopters). On-board avionics enable the crew to accurately navigate by day or night and in all weather conditions. Computer-aided terrain-following flight systems permit low-altitude operation. To locate targets, the crew use an

ABOVE: **The configuration of the Mil Mi-28 is essentially the same as other attack helicopters. The use of a tail wheel-type undercarriage allows a gun and mounting to be positioned under the cockpit.**

ABOVE: **The Mil Mi-28 can carry the B-8 pod, which contains 80mm folding-fin unguided missiles and eight AT-9 anti-tank missiles on each stub wing.**

LEFT: **A Shipunov 30mm 2A42 cannon is positioned in a mounting under the forward fuselage.**

infra-red imaging and target search radar – the sight is mounted on a mast above the rotor head to allow the helicopter to be held at the hover below a tree line or buildings, not exposed to enemy fire. Radar and laser illumination warning systems alert the crew to any enemy radar threat or heat-seeking missile attack.

The helicopter is powered by two Klimov TV-3-117VMA turboshaft engines mounted in pods above each wing root for protection against ground fire. Manufactured from composite materials, the downward deflecting nozzles shroud the engine exhausts to minimize the heat signature. The cockpit is compatible with Night Vision Goggles (NVG), and the sensor package includes a laser rangefinder and optical sights for weapon aiming.

The cockpit is protected by titanium and ceramic armour, and the window glass can withstand hits from 12.7mm ammunition. At the trailing edge of the port wing, a hatch provides access to a compartment with space for three personnel. The Mi-28 is a helicopter designed to be air-portable and is often transported in Antonov An-22 and Ilyushin Il-76 aircraft of the Russian Air Force.

The first two prototypes were delivered to the military in 2004 for testing. In 2006, the first production Mil Mi-28N was delivered to the Russian military. By early 2012, there were 52 operational, and the type is now the standard attack helicopter in Russian service.

In 2010, it was announced that Venezuela plan to purchase ten machines (Mi-28N-MMW) to equip

the air force as part of a major arms agreement with the Russian government. The type has also been procured by Kenya for service with the air force.

Mil Mi-28

First flight: November 28, 1992
Power: 2 x Klimov TV3-117VMA turboshaft
Armament: 30mm cannon, Ataka-V anti-tank missiles, S-8 rocket, S13 rocket, 23mm Gsh-23L gun pods, Sheksna and 9A-2200 anti-tank missile
Size: Rotor diameter – 17.2m/55ft 1in
Length – 17.01m/55ft 5in
Height – 3.82m/12ft 7in
Weights: Empty – 8,094kg/17,844lb
Take-off – 12,000kg/26,455lb (maximum)
Performance: Speed – 304kph/189mph (maximum)
Service ceiling – 5,700m/10,702ft
Range – 450km/279 miles

NH Industries NH90

The NH90 is a versatile twin-engine helicopter developed by NH Industries (a venture owned by AgustaWestland, Eurocopter and Fokker Technologies) and designed to meet a NATO requirement for a medium multi-role military helicopter that provides the benefits of type standardization for both land and maritime operations. The helicopter is available in two versions, the NATO Frigate Helicopter (NFH) and the Tactical Transport Helicopter (TTH).

The prototype NH90 was first flown on December 18, 1995, and the production TTH helicopter was first flown in May 2004. After a two-year production delay, deliveries of the NH90 began in December 2006, when three TTH transport helicopters were handed over to the German Army. In August 2007, the NFH version was flown for the first time.

The airframe of the NH90 is constructed from composite materials to reduce the number of parts, and

ABOVE: **The NH90 is built in two versions – the NFH for naval operations and the TTH tactical transport.**

structural weight with increased strength, improved fatigue life and resistance to corrosion and battle damage. The blades of the main rotor are also manufactured from composite materials for strength, damage tolerance and improved fatigue life.

The helicopter is equipped with fly-by-wire flight controls with no mechanical back-up, which reduces the overall weight,

LEFT: **An NH90 Tactical Transport Helicopter (TTH) in service with the German Army. The machine is held in the hover, which causes the tips of the main rotor blades to generate vortices in the moist air over the forest.**

LEFT: **The NATO Frigate Helicopter (NFH) version of the NH90 in service with Aéronavale, the air arm of the French Navy. The NFH is built primarily as an Anti-Submarine Warfare (ASW) helicopter, but can be used for many other roles.**

maximizes performance and lessens crew workload. Maintenance and inspection requirements are also greatly reduced compared with those for a conventional control system. In December 2003, the NH90 became the first medium-sized transport helicopter to fly with full fly-by-wire controls. The aircraft has a full glass cockpit, with all flight, aircraft systems and maintenance data being displayed to the crew (in colour) on five multi-function LCD screens. All are compatible with Night Vision Goggles (NVG) and helmet-mounted display systems.

The NH90 is designed to operate in confined spaces such as the deck of a ship (NFH), but has cabin large enough to accommodate 20 fully equipped troops (TTH). The primary role of this version is the transportation of troops, but it can easily be adapted to carry more than 2,500kg/5,511lb of cargo. The type is also equipped for the SAR mission and can be quickly adapted for MEDEVAC/CASEVAC duties to carry up to 12 stretchers. In Finnish and Swedish service, the TTH is designated TTT (Tactical Troop Transport).

The primary missions of the NFH version are in the Anti-Submarine Warfare (ASW) and Anti-Surface unit Warfare (ASuW) roles, and it can be armed with a variety of weapons, including anti-submarine torpedoes, air-to-surface missiles and air-to-air missiles.

On ASW operations, a typical four-hour mission is made up of a 35-minute flight to the area of operation, 20 minutes dropping sonobuoys, two hours on surveillance, 30 minutes releasing torpedoes and 35 minutes for the return flight to the frigate. In a typical four-hour screening operation, the helicopter would take 15 minutes to reach the area of operation, three hours and 30 minutes in the area executing 11 consecutive cycles of ten-minute sonar dipping, then 15 minutes to return to the home ship.

In the anti-surface warfare role, the helicopter is equipped with an Over The Horizon (OTH) capability to detect, track, identify and attack an enemy vessel. Secondary roles include Anti-Air Warfare (AAW), Vertical Replenishment (VertRep), SAR, troop transport and mine laying. The helicopter has a crew of three – a pilot, a Tactical Coordinator (Tacco) responsible for mission management and a Sensor Systems Operator (Senso) – and can be operated day and night and in all weather conditions.

Many of the aircraft being operated in Europe are fitted with a counter-measures and self-protection suite which includes a missile approach warning system, integrated radar warning and laser warning receivers. Chaff and flare dispensers are also standard equipment. Other sensors fitted

include Forward Looking Infra-Red (FLIR), Magnetic Anomaly Detector (MAD) and sonar equipment.

The NFH version is powered by two Rolls-Royce Turboméca RTM322-01/9 turboshaft engines. Those ordered for service with Italian and Spanish forces are powered by General Electric T700/T6E1 turboshaft engines.

Although the NH90 was developed for and is in service with NATO countries, it has been ordered by a number of other countries around the world and is, at the time of writing, in service with the Australian Army and Navy (NH-90 Cobra), Royal New Zealand Air Force, Royal Air Force of Oman (a hot and high version) and the air arms of Finland and Sweden.

NH Industries NH90 NFH

First flight: December 18, 1995
Power: 2 x Rolls-Royce Turboméca RTM322 turboshaft
Armament: Martel Mk2/S anti-ship missile, torpedoes
Size: Rotor diameter – 16.3m/53ft 6in
Length – 19.56m/64ft 2in
Height – 5.31m/16ft 5in
Weights: Empty – 6,400kg/14,109lb
Take-off – 10,600kg/23,369lb (maximum)
Performance: Speed – 300kph/186mph (maximum)
Ceiling – 6,000m/19,686ft
Range – 900km/559 miles

Piasecki YH-16 Transporter

In the post-war years, as the Strategic Air Command (SAC) arm of the USAF was being increased in size and worldwide operations, so grew a requirement for an aircraft to rescue any aircrew shot down or forced to abandon their aircraft far from base. In 1946, the USAF detailed a requirement for a large long-range helicopter for this role, and issued a contract to the Piasecki Helicopter Corporation to build two development machines in 1949. Known to the company as the PV-15, now designated XH-16A (serial number 50-1269), it was first flown on October 23, 1953, with test pilots Harold Peterson and Phil Camerano at the controls.

At the time, the XH-16A was the largest helicopter in the world, and each of the two overlapping rotors had a diameter of 25m/82ft. The fuselage was as capacious as that of a Douglas DC-4 transport aircraft. The YH-16A could carry up to 40 fully equipped troops or three light trucks loaded into the aircraft up a ramp through a rear door.

The helicopter (officially named Transporter) was initially powered by two Pratt & Whitney R-2180-11 radial piston engines and was the world's first twin-engine helicopter. First flown in 1955, the YH-16A (the Y prefix denotes an experimental aircraft) was powered by two Allison YT38-A-10 turboshaft engines and was the first helicopter in the world to be powered in this way. The three blades of each rotor were assembled from a milled aluminium outer skin, an aluminium honeycomb core and a leading edge balance weight which acted as a form of mechanical fastener. The slow rotating speed (125rpm) of the rotors made the blades almost visible when turning. Each engine drove an individual rotor. The proposed YH-16B was to have been powered by two Allison YT56-A5-2 turboshaft engines and to transport up to 69 passengers. One development designed by Piasecki for the YH-16B was a large load-carrying pod fitted under the fuselage to carry equipment. This required the undercarriage to be lengthened.

Although impressive, the helicopter was underpowered and lacked the

ABOVE: **The US Air Force tested the Piasecki YH-16, but the programme was abandoned after the crash of the second prototype. Various pods were designed for special functions, including a field operating room, an electronics centre and a mobile repair centre.**

required performance. The USAF decided against procuring the YH-16A, but the US Army continued testing the machine until the second XH-16A suffered a catastrophic mechanical failure, broke up and crashed in December 1956.

Piasecki XH-16A Transporter

First flight: October 23, 1953
Power: 2 x Pratt & Whitney R 2180-11 radial piston engines
Armament: None
Size: Rotor diameter – 25m/82ft
  Length – 23.79m/78ft
  Height – 7.62m/25ft
Weights: Empty – 14,534kg/32,041lb
  Take-off – 20,893kg/46,060lb (maximum)
Performance: Speed – 198kph/123mph (maximum)
  Ceiling – 5,490m/18,000ft
  Range – 370km/230 miles

LEFT: **For ease of maintenance, the fuselage was designed to allow the engine and mounting, fan cowling and oil system to be removed as a single unit through a roof hatch. The HUP-2 entered service with the US Navy and US Marine Corps in 1949.**

Piasecki HUP Retriever/UH-25 Army Mule

In 1945, US Navy Board of Aeronautics issued a specification for a helicopter suitable for operations from aircraft carriers, battleships or cruisers and other large vessels in the US Fleet. The Piasecki Helicopter Corporation and Sikorsky Aircraft Corporation were issued with contracts to design and build prototypes. After evaluation, the Sikorsky XHJS-1 was cancelled and Piasecki were contracted to build two prototypes designated XHJP-1 (Model PV-14).

The XHJP-1 was first flown in March 1948. After extensive trials, the HUP-1 Retriever (Model PV-18) entered production for the US Navy. In 1949, the type began to enter USN service, and in February 1951 the first operational aircraft were in service with Helicopter Utility Squadron 2 (HU-2) "Fleet Angels" as part of Carrier Group Six. The aircraft was powered by a Continental R975-46 radial piston engine driving overlapping tandem rotors. The HUP-1 had a two-man crew and could accommodate up to five passengers or three stretchers. By 1952, Piasecki had delivered 32 of the type to the USN.

The second production version was the HUP-2, which had the more powerful Continental R975-46A engine and was the first production helicopter to be fitted with a Sperry-manufactured auto-pilot. The HUP-2S was equipped with dipping sonar equipment for anti-submarine warfare operations. The HUP-2S was found to be underpowered for the demanding ASW role, resulting in the sonar equipment being removed and the aircraft being used for SAR and transport missions.

A total of 193 were built, of which 15 were supplied to France for service with the navy.

A version of the HUP-2 was developed for the US Army and designated H-25A Army Mule (UH-25C in 1962). This model was fitted with large doors and power-boosted controls, as well as a strengthened cabin floor to carry a heavier payload. A total of 70 were delivered from 1953, but were judged to be unsuitable for front-line deployment. Consequently, from 1955, a total of 50 machines were transferred to the USN and designated HUP-3. The Navy was already operating a number of Retrievers which had been upgraded to HUP-3 standard. By 1958, those that remained on the US Army inventory were used for training purposes and withdrawn from service. The Royal Canadian Navy (RCN) also took delivery of three HUP-3s.

During the Korean War, the type was used extensively for transport and rescue missions by US forces. A total of 339 had been built when the production line was closed in July 1954. The type was finally withdrawn from service in 1964.

LEFT: **The Piasecki HUP-3 Retriever was fitted with a large rectangular hatch, offset to the right, to allow a rescue winch with a capacity of up to 181kg/399lb to be operated.**

Piasecki HUP-3 Retriever

First flight: March, 1948
Power: 1 x Continental R-975-46A radial piston engine
Armament: None
Size: Rotor diameter – 10.67m/35ft
　　Length – 17.35m/56ft 11in
　　Height – 3.84m/12ft 7in
Weights: Empty – 1,786kg/3,938lb
　　Take-off – 2,767kg/6,100lb (maximum)
Performance: Speed – 169kph/105mph (maximum)
　　Ceiling – 3,048m/10,000ft
　　Range – 547km/340 miles

Piasecki H-21 Workhorse/Shawnee

The H-21 was developed from the all-metal HRP-2 which, in turn, was a development of the HRP-1 Rescuer, the original "Flying Banana" flown by the US Navy, US Marine Corps and US Coast Guard. It was the fourth tandem rotor machine designed by the Piasecki Helicopter Corporation to enter production for the United States military.

The helicopter was designed in response to a United States Air Force (USAF) specification for a helicopter to operate in the long-range rescue role in Arctic conditions. The XH-21 was first flown on April 11, 1952. The USAF,

having already ordered 18 pre-production YH-21As in 1949 for evaluation, placed a production order for 32, designated H-21A Workhorse. They were to serve in the search and rescue role with the Military Air Transport Service Air Rescue (MATSAR). The first production H-21A flew in October 1953, and a further six aircraft were built for the Canadian military under the Military Assistance Program (MAP) to be deployed in support of the DEW (Distant Early Warning) line radar installations across the Canadian Arctic.

ABOVE: **A pre-production YH-21A flight test machine being flown for the first time in front of a crowd of Piasecki employees.**

The second version to be developed was the H-21B Workhorse for the USAF Troop Carrier Command (TCC). This aircraft was fitted with an uprated Curtis-Wright R-1820-103 Cyclone radial piston engine, the rotor blades were extended by 15cm/6in, and it was equipped with a Sperry autopilot. The machine had a significantly higher maximum take-off weight and could accommodate 20 fully equipped troops or 12 stretchers in the CASEVAC role. The H-21B was operated by the USN (10) and by the Japanese Self-Defense Force (JSDF), which also had 10 in service.

The US Army version of the H-21B was designated H-21C Shawnee (CH-21C after July 1962). A number of these machines were exported to the French Army (98) and Navy (10), Canada (6) and to the then West Germany (32). The C model was fitted with a large hook under the fuselage to enable a load of up to 1,814kg/4,000lb to be lifted.

LEFT: **Although the Piasecki H-21B was developed for long-range rescue operations, the type could be used to lift loads such as a light military vehicle.**

LEFT: **The Piasecki H-21C Workhorse was fitted with two external auxiliary tanks when being deployed for a long-range rescue mission. Six of the type were supplied to the Royal Canadian Air Force (RCAF) to be used as support aircraft for the Distant Early Warning (DEW) line of radar installations sited across northern Canada.**

In the mid-1950s, French forces were embroiled in the Algerian War, and both the French Air Force and Army were keen to explore the use of the helicopter in the ground-attack role. As a result, some of their H-21Cs were trialled on the battlefront with fixed, forward-firing machine-guns and rockets. A few were trialled with bomb racks fitted, but the machine's manoeuvrability and performance were found to be unsuitable for ground-attack. The H-21C continued to be used as a troop transport by French forces. Most were fitted with a door-mounted machine-gun or 20mm cannon for self-defence during high-risk ground operations. The French military

also found that the Shawnee was less vulnerable to ground fire due to the location of the fuel tanks. Although not suited for ground-attack, by the end of the Algerian War the French had developed very effective large-scale counter-insurgency tactics, in which the H-21C Shawnee troop transports were deployed alongside ground-attack Sikorsky H-34 Choctaws.

The US Army also explored the potential of the H-21C as a gunship or ground-attack helicopter, either armed with machine-guns mounted under the nose or with a gun mounting in each door opening. In US Army service, the H-21C was, however, most extensively used as a troop or supply transport. In August 1954, a US Army H-21C named "Amblin' Annie" became the first helicopter to be flown non-stop across

the USA, being refuelled in flight via a very basic hose system trailed from a de Havilland (Canada) U-1A Otter.

After Vertol acquired Piasecki in 1959, Sweden ordered two of the Model 44 (civilian H-21B) helicopters for their air force and nine of the same machines for the navy.

In December 1961, the H-21C Shawnee was deployed to South-east Asia for service with the 8th and 57th Transportation Companies of the US Army. Relatively low speed and unprotected control cables and fuel lines made the H-21C vulnerable to ground fire. In Vietnam, despite some early losses, the type provided the US Army with a reliable supply and transport helicopter until 1964, when it was replaced with the Bell UH-1 Iroquois. All Piasecki CH-21 helicopters in US military service had been retired by the end of 1964.

BELOW: **The H-21 was an early successful example of a multi-role helicopter, and could land on wheels, skis or floats.**

Piasecki CH-21C Shawnee

First flight: April 11, 1952
Power: 1 x Curtis-Wright R-1820-103 Cyclone radial piston engine
Armament: None
Size: Rotor diameter – 13.41m/44ft
Length – 26.31m/86ft 4in
Height – 4.70m/15ft 5in
Weights: Empty – 3,629kg/8,000lb
Take-off – 6,668kg/14,700lb (maximum)
Performance: Speed – 211kph/131mph (maximum)
Service ceiling – 2,360m/7,750ft
Range – 644km/400 miles

LEFT: **This R-4B serial 43-46506 is preserved at the National Museum of the United States Air Force at Dayton, Ohio.**

Sikorsky R-4

The Vought-Sikorsky VS-300 experimental helicopter was a pioneering design, being the first to be fitted with cyclic controls for the rotor and an anti-torque tail rotor. The prototype was first flown in tethered flight on September 14, 1939, with Igor Sikorsky at the controls. On May 13, 1940, the VS-300 was free-flown by Sikorsky for the first time. Continued success with flight trials resulted in a commitment by the United States Army Air Forces (USAAF), in 1941, to proceed with the development of the XR-4 (X – Experimental, R – Rotorcraft).

The fuselage was constructed from steel tubing that was covered almost entirely with fabric. The rotor blades were of conventional spar and rib construction, also covered with fabric. The enclosed cockpit had side-by-side seating accommodation for a crew of two and had dual controls. The XR-4 was first flown on January 14, 1942, powered by a Warner R-500-1 Super Scarab radial piston engine.

In May 1942, serial number 41-18874, was flown 1,225km/761 miles in stages from Bridgeport, Connecticut to Wright Field, Ohio in just over 16 hours. The XR-4 went on to break all previous helicopter endurance, altitude and speed records. The US Army was sufficiently impressed to order 29 pre-production machines for evaluation in January 1943. Designated YR-4, all were fitted with the more powerful Warner R-550-3 engine and lengthened rotor blades. Evaluation of these machines led to further improvements, including an increased fuel capacity. The tailwheel was moved further to the rear of the tail boom to improve stability on the ground. These machines were designated YR-4B.

In 1943, one of the pre-production machines was used to execute the first-ever landing of a helicopter on a ship at sea, when being operated from the deck of USS *Bunker Hill* (CV-17).

In April 1944, a YR-4B flown by US Army pilot Lt Carter Harman was deployed to carry out the very first helicopter combat rescue. In the humid, high-altitude conditions of Burma, Lt Harman rescued the pilot and three passengers from a USAAF

BELOW: **The more streamlined R-6 was known as the HOS-1 or Hoverfly II. Note the wheel mounted underneath the tail boom root, to keep the tail rotor well clear of the ground.**

RIGHT: **In British service, the R-4 was known as the Hoverfly. The fuselage was a space frame constructed from steel tubing and covered with fabric. The end of the tail boom was left uncovered to allow access to the tail rotor assembly.**

liaison aircraft that had landed in the jungle. It took four flights as only one passenger could be carried at a time, but all were airlifted to safety. Lt Harman was only the seventh US Army pilot to be helicopter-qualified. Over the following weeks, he flew another 15 jungle rescue missions.

Six ships of the US Navy (USN), each carrying two YR-4B helicopters, were sent to the South Pacific to serve as floating Aviation Repair Units (ARU) for damaged US aircraft. When not

BELOW: **The Sikorsky R-6A was operated by the US Navy as the HOS-1. The type was also used by British military services as the Hoverfly II.**

required for parts delivery flights, the helicopters were available for MEDEVAC duties. In 1948, all of the R-4Bs remaining in US service were redesignated H-4B.

The first production (R-4B) batch of 100 machines was fitted with the more powerful Warner R-550-3 engine. Of these, 35 were delivered to the USAAF for liaison and observation duties. The US Navy took delivery of 20 designated HNS-1 for reconnaissance, transport and air sea rescue duties. The Royal Navy had been very interested in development of the type and had received some YR-4B pre-production machines for evaluation. By the end of the World War II, there were

a number of development and production machines in Great Britain, including 45 production machines supplied under the Lend-Lease Programme. In Royal Air Force service, where it was known as the Hoverfly I, the type was flown by the Helicopter Training School at RAF Andover, Hampshire, No. 529 Squadron at RAF Henley-on-Thames, Oxfordshire, and was operated by The King's Flight from RAF Benson in Oxfordshire. The Fleet Air Arm (FAA) of the Royal Navy was the main operator of the type. The Hoverfly I remained in service into the mid-1950s, with the Joint Experimental Helicopter Unit (JHEU) established on April 1, 1955.

First flown on October 15, 1943, the R-6 was an improved version with a streamlined part metal fuselage and a more powerful Franklin 0-405-9 piston engine. In USN service the R-6 was designated HOS-1, and in British service as the Hoverfly II.

Sikorsky R-4B

First flight: January 14, 1942 (XR-4)
Power: 1 x Warner R-550-3 Super Scarab radial piston engine
Armament: None
Size: Rotor diameter – 11.6m/38ft 1in
Length – 14.65m/48ft 1in
Height – 3.78m/12ft 5in
Weights: Empty – 952kg/2,098lb
Take-off – 1,171kg/2,581lb (maximum)
Performance: Speed – 120kph/75mph (maximum)
Service ceiling – 2,438m/8,000ft
Range – 209km/130 miles

Sikorsky S-51

Building on the confidence gained from the R-4 helicopter and responding to a United States Army Air Forces requirement for a far more capable machine, Sikorsky Aircraft Corporation developed the VS-337, a two-seater helicopter powered by a radial engine. Designated XR-5, the type was powered by a Pratt & Whitney R-985 Wasp Junior radial piston engine, and was flown for the first time on August 18, 1943. After a successful test programme, the helicopter entered service with the USAAF as the H-5. The US Navy procured the HO2S, and the US Coast Guard the HO3S. The type was to become widely known as the Sikorsky model number S-51.

In US Army service, the H-5 was used for spotting and communications work, but it is perhaps best known as a rescue aircraft during the Korean War. The S-51 afforded the military a new means of extracting personnel from behind enemy lines or from the sea. Early H-5s were fitted with a litter (stretcher) carrier on each side for casualty evacuation duties and, later, a rescue hoist. This allowed battlefield casualties to be recovered rapidly and transported for medical treatment.

RIGHT: **Survivability in the event of an emergency water landing was a key consideration in the development of the type.**

On November 29, 1945, the first successful air sea rescue by helicopter was carried out by test pilot Dimitry Viner flying an H-5 when he lifted two seamen to safety from a sinking ship, a short distance from the Sikorsky plant in Stanford, Connecticut. The last H-5 and HO3S-1 helicopters were retired from active US military service in 1957. US production lasted until 1951, by which time Sikorsky had built a total of 285.

ABOVE: **The success of the Dragonfly gave Westland the confidence to adapt and develop other Sikorsky designs. The British company rapidly developed into a major helicopter manufacturer.**

In 1946, Westland Aircraft Limited negotiated a licence agreement with Sikorsky that led to production of the type in the UK. The first Westland-built S-51 was flown for the first time in 1948. The S-51 Dragonfly was an

almost complete redesign by Westland and was powered by a British-built Alvis Leonides radial piston engine. In 1953, production ceased after 139 machines had been completed. The Dragonfly was the first UK-built helicopter to enter service with the British military. The Royal Navy was the first UK military operator with the HR.1, an Air Sea Rescue (ASR) version. The first RN squadron to fly the Dragonfly was No.705 Naval Air Squadron (NAS) formed at Royal Naval Air Station Gosport (HMS Siskin), near Portsmouth. The rescue version of the type was equipped with a powered hoist with a lifting capacity of 170kg/375lb.

The HC.2 operated by the Royal Air Force was similar to the RN version but fitted with carriers for the casualty evacuation role. The prime ASR version in Royal Navy service was the HR.3, and a total of 58 were built. This machine and the HC.4 in RAF service were fitted with all-metal rotor blades and hydraulic servo-assisted controls.

ABOVE: **A US Navy Sikorsky HO3-S1 parked in front of a Royal Air Force Handley-Page Hastings transport aircraft.**

During the Malaya Emergency, RAF machines were deployed on operations from 1950, and in three and a half years the type was used to evacuate 675 casualties, transport over 4,000 passengers and move 38,100kg/84,000lb of supplies in some 6,000 sorties.

The Widgeon was developed from the Dragonfly by Westland as a private venture, but although it was an excellent machine, only a small number (15) were built.

The Sikorsky S-51 and the Westland Dragonfly were exported to Argentina, Australia, Belgium, Brazil, Canada, Ceylon, Egypt, France, Iraq, Italy, Japan, the Philippines, Thailand and Yugoslavia.

An early pre-production YH-5A, serial number 43-46620, is preserved at the National Museum of the US Air Force at Wright Patterson Air Force Base in Ohio.

ABOVE: **A Westland S-51 Dragonfly during flight trials with stretcher-carrying panniers mounted on each side of the aircraft. The type was used operationally by the RAF.**

Sikorsky S-51

First flight: August 18, 1943 (XR-5)
Power: Pratt & Whitney radial piston engine
Armament: None
Size: Rotor diameter – 14.63m/48ft
Length – 17.4m/57ft 1in
Height – 3.96m/13ft
Weights: Empty – 1,718kg/3,780lb
Take-off –2,193kg/4,825lb (maximum)
Performance: Speed – 171kph/106mph (maximum)
Service ceiling – 4,390m/14,400ft
Range – 580km/360 miles

Sikorsky H-19 Chickasaw

In May 1949, the Sikorsky Aircraft Corporation was given what appeared to be the impossible task of designing an all-new helicopter for the US Air Force in just seven months. The new machine, Sikorsky model S-55, had to carry ten passengers as well as a crew of two. The task was achieved, and on November 10, 1949, the first of five YH-19 prototypes was flown for the first time. The YH-19 was the first large helicopter manufactured by the company, and was to remain in military service into the 1990s.

After successful trials, the USAF ordered a batch of 55, designated H-19A and fitted with the same Pratt & Whitney R-1340-57 Wasp radial piston engine used to power the prototype machines. On this and all later models, the engine was accessed through distinctive clamshell doors, which made routine servicing a relatively easy task – an engine change would take just two hours. The location of the engine in the nose allowed the cockpit to be positioned at the centre of gravity, thereby allowing a range of loads to be carried within the helicopter without stability being affected.

RIGHT: **Each of the four legs on the wide stable undercarriage was fitted with a shock absorber for maximum stability during take-off, landing and taxiing. Floats could be fitted or permanent amphibious landing gear could be installed.**

The engine was linked to the main rotor gearbox by a long drive-shaft.

Ease of maintenance and versatility were fundamental to the design of the machine. For example, each undercarriage leg was fitted with an independent shock absorber which improved stability during landing and take-off.

The S-55 was of pod-and-boom design, and was constructed with the extensive use of magnesium and aluminium to reduce the structural weight and therefore enhance performance. Early examples can be identified by the lack of a distinctive triangular-shaped fillet where the tail boom meets the fuselage, and by the

ABOVE: **The YH-19 prototype lacked the triangular fillet that connected the fuselage to the tail boom, which featured in production machines. The prototype's horizontal stabilizer on the starboard side of the tail was replaced by two anhedral fins in production machines.**

addition of the inverted fins on the underside of the tail boom – these were fitted to improve lateral stability.

Production continued for the USAF, with 270 examples of the H-19B powered by the Wright R-1300-3 Cyclone radial piston engine driving a larger-diameter main rotor. An order for 72 of the H-19C followed from the US Army and, following tradition, the type was named Chickasaw. In 1962,

ABOVE: **The Sikorsky H-19B was powered by a Wright R-1300-3 Cyclone radial piston engine driving a larger-diameter main rotor.**

ABOVE: **The engine on the S-55 was mounted at an angle in the nose behind clamshell doors for easy servicing. The drive-shaft to the gearbox ran through the cabin.**

under the Department of Defense (DoD) directive, the type was redesignated UH-19C and UH-19D. The type was the first transport helicopter to enter service with the US Army.

The US Navy also procured versions of the S-55, having signed a contract in April 1950. Between 1950 and 1958, the USN took delivery of 119, including ten HO4S-1 (H-19A) and 61 of the HO4S-2 (30 of these were built for the US Coast Guard as the HO4S-3G). The US Marine Corps received 90 of the HRS-2 and 84 of the HRS-3, which were used as troop transports and built to the same specification as the HO4S. Although the SAR variant was deployed by the USN towards the end of the Korean War and saw limited service, the USMC gained operational experience with the type on assault missions. The UH-19 Chickasaw

remained in service during the early years of the Vietnam War.

In Korea, the type proved to be so versatile that it allowed the US military the opportunity to develop various operational techniques, including landing troops in enemy territory, transport and recovery of damaged vehicles, moving equipment and for aircrew rescue. On September 13, 1951, helicopters were used for the first time to transport troops into combat when US Marines were deployed to a hill under attack by Chinese forces. In the CASEVAC role, up to six stretchers could be accommodated.

In March 1952, the type was certified for civilian operations and offered in two versions, the S-55A powered by a Pratt & Whitney R-1340 Cyclone radial piston engine and the S-55B powered by a

Wright R-1300-3 Wasp radial piston engine. Later that year, the type was flown by Sabena, the national airline of Belgium, on the first commercial rotary wing services when the type was operated between Belgium, the Netherlands, France and Germany.

A total of 1,067 of all military versions built were operated by the air services of some 30 nations. In the UK, Westland Aircraft built 547 under licence. Licence production was also carried out in France by SNCA, and many of these machines were used by French forces during the war in Algeria.

ABOVE: **The US Marine Corps used the type to develop air assault operations in the Korean War. The type went on to serve for a short period in Vietnam.**

Sikorsky H-19B Chickasaw

First flight: November 10, 1949
Power: 1 x Wright R-1300-3 Wasp
   radial piston engine
Armament: None
Size: Rotor diameter – 16.16m/53ft
   Length – 12.85m/42ft 2in
   Height – 4.07m/13ft 3in
Weights: Empty – 2,381kg/5,250lb
   Take-off – 3,583kg/7,900lb (maximum)
Performance: Speed – 180kph/112mph (maximum)
   Service ceiling – 3,940m/13,000ft
   Range – 580km/360 miles

Sikorsky CH-37 Mojave

The Sikorsky CH-37 Mojave (company designation S-56) was the first heavy-lift helicopter built for the US Marine Corps, and was for a decade the largest helicopter flying outside of the Soviet Union. Until late 1961, the CH-37 was the largest helicopter in the US military inventory.

The type was produced to meet a USMC requirement for an assault helicopter with the capacity to transport 26 fully equipped troops, and was the first twin-engine type designed by Sikorsky.

The machine was powered by two Pratt & Whitney R-2800 Double Wasp radial piston engines of the type used by many World War II combat aircraft. The engines were not positioned inside the fuselage but were fitted in nacelles, which also housed the retractable main undercarriage, mounted on stub wings. If gunfire hit the five-blade rotor main rotor, it was designed to continue providing lift with one blade missing. For transportation, the main rotor blades were folded back along the top of the

ABOVE: **For many years, the Sikorsky CH-37A Mojave was the largest helicopter in service with the US military forces.**

fuselage. A large four-blade anti-torque rotor was mounted at the tail. This was a unique approach to designing a heavy-lift helicopter. The XHR2S-1 prototype was first flown on December 18, 1953.

The engine arrangement gave an unobstructed cargo area in the fuselage, and up to three jeep-type light vehicles loaded through large clamshell doors in the nose could be transported. Alternatively, up to 907kg/2,000lb of cargo could be carried. Two 1,136-litre/300-gallon auxiliary fuel tanks containing extra fuel for the engines were mounted flush with the fuselage in line with the undercarriage.

The US Army had also evaluated the prototype in 1954, and were sufficiently impressed to order 94 machines designated H-37A Mojave. Deliveries to the 4th Medium Helicopter Transportation Company (MHTC) began in 1958, and all deliveries were completed by mid-1960. All US Army

LEFT: **The CH-37B Mojave was fitted with an auto-stabilizer system manufactured by Lear.**

machines were later upgraded to
B standard by the installation of crash-
proof fuel tanks and auto-stabilization
equipment manufactured by Lear, which
allowed the H-37A to be loaded and
unloaded while held in the hover.

In 1962, all military aircraft in
US service were given standardized
designations, and under this system
the type became the CH-37C.

Two machines in US Navy
service were converted to HR2S-1W
configuration by fitting an AN/APS-20E

radar scanner in a radome mounted
under the nose for evaluation for Airborne
Early Warning (AEW) operations. Airframe
vibration was a severe problem, and the
trials were cancelled.

In 1963, the US Army briefly deployed
four CH-37Bs to Vietnam for the
recovery, often from behind enemy lines,
of downed US aircraft. The CH-37 had
a comparatively short service life, being
phased out in the late 1960s. All of the
type were replaced in US Army service
with the Sikorsky CH-54 Tarhe, a lighter

ABOVE: **The engines the CH-37 Mojave were
mounted in nacelles which also housed the
retractable undercarriage.**

machine powered by two turboshaft
engines, which had a lifting capacity
five times greater than the CH-37.

In developing the CH-37 Mojave,
the Sikorsky team gained valuable
experience which they were able to use
in the design and production of later
large single-rotor helicopters for the US
military. Total production of the CH-37,
including prototypes, amounted to
150 airframes, 94 delivered to the
US Army and 55 to the USMC.

ABOVE: **The CH-37 Mojave was used to transport light vehicles and troops, as well as to carry larger
items, including light aircraft as an under-slung load. The type was the last large helicopter to be
piston engine-powered.**

Sikorsky CH-37B Mojave

First flight: December 18, 1953
Power: 2 x Pratt & Whitney R-2800-54
Double Wasp radial piston engines
Armament: None
Size: Rotor diameter – 21.95m/72ft
Length – 19.59m/64ft 3in
Height – 6.71m/22ft
Weights: Empty – 9,449kg/20,831lb
Take-off –14,090kg/31,063lb (maximum)
Performance: Speed – 209kph/130mph (maximum)
Service ceiling – 2,650m/8,700ft
Range – 233km/145 miles

Sikorsky H-34 Choctaw

The Sikorsky H-34 (company model S-58) was originally designed for anti-submarine warfare, later serving in transport and firefighting, rescue of astronauts, disaster recovery and even flying presidents. The machine was flown for the first time on March 8, 1954, and in September of that year the first of them entered service with the US Navy, initially designated HSS-1 Seabat (anti-submarine) and HUS-1 Seahorse (transport). The USN designations for the type included those in service with the US Marine Corps and US Coast Guard. In 1962, a Department of Defense (DoD) common designation system for US military aircraft was introduced, and the H-34 became the SH-34 Seabat, the UH-34 Seahorse and the CH-34 Choctaw.

The Sikorsky H-34 was built as a larger, more powerful single-engine successor to the H-19 Chickasaw and was one of the last piston-engined helicopters to enter service with the military.

ABOVE: **The Sikorsky S-58 was sold to military and civilian operators around the world. The US Marine Corps (USMC) operated the type as the HUS-1 and UH-34D.**

The USN machines were used for the recovery of capsules and astronauts during the NASA Mercury space programme. An SH-34G Seabat rescued Alan B. Shepard, Jr. from the sea after his historic suborbital flight in 1961. Later in the same year, the hatch on the Mercury 4 capsule opened too early and the capsule filled with water. Although the Seabat was renowned for an excellent weight-lifting capability, the capsule, Liberty Bell 7, proved too heavy and it was released and sank beneath the waves.

The airframe of the CH-34 used magnesium in the structure, and as this is a particularly flammable metal, the type was therefore vulnerable to ground fire. This is perhaps one of reasons that the US Army never deployed any of the type to Vietnam, choosing to operate the Piasecki CH-21 Shawnee before the introduction into service of the Bell UH-1 Iroquois. Ironically, however, a number of the type had been sold

LEFT: **A damaged Cessna L-19 Bird Dog liason and observation aircraft being attached to a Sikorsky CH-34 Choctaw. The lifting capability was impressive.**

LEFT: **A Sikorsky UH-34D Seahorse viewed over South Vietnam from the door gunner's position of an accompanying UH-34D. Both helicopters are from Marine Medium Transport Squadron 162 (HMM-162). The aircraft is armed with a 7.62mm M60 machine-gun.**
ABOVE: **A US Army CH-34C Choctaw in flight.**

to the Army of the Republic of Vietnam (ARV), although it is reported they were not widely used due to a lack of spare parts and maintenance problems. However, despite being phased out of US Army service, the USMC continued to use the CH-34 even after the Tet Offensive in 1968. The H-34 was highly regarded by USMC aircrews, who liked the aircraft's simplicity and reliability – so much so that the phrase "give me a HUS" or "cut me a HUS" came to mean "help me out" in common Marine parlance, referring to the HUS Seahorse. All H-34s were retired from US military service by the early 1970s.

In June 1967, the CH-34 was deployed to great effect during the Israeli Six-Days War. In 1959, Israel received 24 S-58s (the civil variant of the H-34), which had been originally intended for West Germany but diverted to the Levant. By 1967, the Israeli Air Force had No.124 (Rolling Sword) Squadron established with a complement of 28 aircraft. As the war continued over the week of June 5–10, these helicopters went from merely evacuating stranded pilots after a crash to dropping Israeli paratroops behind enemy lines to capture Sharm-El-Sheik in Egypt, as well as the Golan Heights in Syria.

Although the piston Choctaws were only in military use for about 20 years, they were manufactured under licence in both France and in the United Kingdom as the Westland Wessex.

ABOVE: **A number of CH-34 airframes were remanufactured and converted to turbine power for military and civilian operators as the T-58. The fuselage was lengthened and fitted with a Pratt & Whitney Canada PT6T-3 Twin-Pac turboshaft engine installation.**

Sikorsky H-34A Choctaw

First flight: March 8, 1954
Power: 1 x Wright R-1820-84 radial piston engine
Armament: Machine-gun, rockets
Size: Rotor diameter – 17.0m/56ft
    Length of fuselage – 17.27m/56ft 7in
    Height – 4.85m/15ft 11in
Weights: Empty – 3,583kg/7,900lb
    Take-off – 6,350kg/14,000lb (maximum)
Performance: Speed – 198kph/123mph (maximum)
    Service ceiling – 2,900m/9,515ft
    Range – 397km/250 miles

Sikorsky SH-3 Sea King

In 1957, the Sikorsky Aircraft Corporation was awarded a contract to design and develop an all-weather amphibious helicopter for the US Navy. The Sikorsky XHSS-2 (company model S-61) was flown for the first time on March 11, 1959. In 1962, the company received an order to build seven YHSS-2 development aircraft. A production order for 245 machines was placed, and the HSS-2 became operational with the USN in June 1961. In 1962, under a directive from the Department of Defense (DoD), the type was designated SH-3.

The SH-3 was powered by two General Electric T58-GE-10 turboshaft engines driving a five-blade main rotor and a conventional tail rotor.

For transport and stowage, the main rotor folded back along the fuselage. The tail boom also folded. The lower fuselage (hull) was boat-shaped to allow amphibious operation. A sponson on each side housed the retractable main undercarriage and inflatable flotation bags. A 272kg/600lb capacity rescue winch is mounted above the main door. In the transport role the SH-3 can accommodate 28 fully equipped troops, and in the SAR role up to 22 passengers or nine stretchers and

SIKORSKY SH-3 SEA KING

ABOVE: **A Brazilian Navy SH-3 Sea King and an SH-3H from Helicopter Anti-Submarine Squadron 9 (HS-9). Dipping sonar is being lowered from both machines during a joint anti-submarine warfare exercise.**

two attendants can be carried. A load of 3,630kg/8,003lb can be lifted by an automatic touchdown release cargo hook mounted under the fuselage.

The Sea King was primarily developed to locate and attack submarines of the Soviet Navy. The aircraft was unique in that it could carry both Anti-Submarine Warfare (ASW) detection equipment and the weapons to attack – a mission that normally required two aircraft. The SH-3 was equipped with AQS-13B/E dipping sonar, ARR-75 sonobuoy receiver, ASQ-81 Magnetic Anomaly Detector (MAD) and an AKT-22 data link. The ASW dipping sonar is lowered through a hatch in the hull. An "attitude-hold" autopilot and sonar coupler link to a radar altimeter, and Doppler radar are fitted to allow the aircraft to be hovered at the exact altitude over a target. In the anti-submarine role, the SH-3 is armed with Mk 44/46 torpedoes and even the B-57 nuclear depth charge. The Sea Eagle or Exocet missile is carried for attack against enemy shipping.

The SH-3A is flown by US Marine Corps unit HMX-1 to operate transport flights under the call sign "Marine One", for the President of the United States. A replacement for the SH-3A is currently being sought under the VXX programme.

The type has been operated by many military forces, including those of Argentina, Brazil, Denmark, India, Iran, Iraq, Malaysia, Peru, Saudia Arabia and Spain. In 2012, the Sea King remains in military service with 17 countries around the world.

The Canadian military procured 41 machines to be assembled by United Aircraft of Canada and designated CH-124. The Sea King was built under licence in Italy by Agusta as the AS-61 and by Mitsubishi, again under licence, in Japan as the S-61. Westland Helicopters obtained a licence to produce the type in the UK and went on to develop a UK Sea King.

Between 1959 and 1980, Sikorsky built some 800 of the type in a number of variants for the military and civilian markets.

ABOVE: **The type was built under licence in Italy by Agusta as the AS-61 for the Italian Navy. For stowage on board a ship, the main rotor blades can be folded back, and part of the tail boom also folds to reduce space.**

Sikorsky SH-3H Sea King

First flight: March 11, 1959
Power: 2 x General Electric T58-GE-10 turboshaft
Armament: Depth charges, anti-shipping missiles, torpedoes
Size: Rotor diameter – 18.9m/62ft
    Length overall – 22.15m/72ft 8in
    Height – 5.13m/16ft 9in
Weights: Empty – 4,428kg/9,762lb
    Take-off – 9,526kg/21,000lb (maximum)
Performance: Speed – 267kph/166mph (maximum)
    Service ceiling – 4,481m/14,700ft
    Range – 1000km/621 miles

Sikorsky HH-3E Jolly Green Giant

The S-61R helicopter was derived from the CH-3 (S-61) Sea King which had been in service with the US Navy since 1961. In 1958, the Sikorsky Aircraft Corporation began design and development of the type as a private venture. The fuselage was redesigned to be much larger, with a rear cargo door and a loading ramp. The lower fuselage was boat-shaped, as on the SH-3, and manufactured to be watertight. On June 17, 1963, the prototype S-61R was flown for the first time. Before the development flying programme was completed, the US Air Force placed an order for 22 aircraft, designated CH-3C, to be operated by rescue and recovery squadrons. A total of 133 were built.

The USAF ordered 42 of the CH-3E, an improved version for long-range rescue missions, and also 41 of the earlier CH-3C were remanufactured to CH-3E specification. Eventually all of these machines would be converted to HH-3E standard. The USAF then purchased 50 of the HH-3E version for specialized Combat Search and Rescue (CSAR) operations in South-east Asia. The MH-3E was a specifically equipped version for missions operated by US Special Forces.

In August 1965, the US Coast Guard (USCG) ordered 40 of the HH-3F version equipped with AN/APN-195 search radar for all-weather Air Sea Rescue (ASR) operations. USCG crews operating the HH-3F named the type "Pelican".

TOP: A Sikorsky HH-3E Jolly Green Giant is the specialized version built for Combat Search and Rescue (CSAR) operations. ABOVE: An early production Sikorsky CH-53E Jolly Green Giant on a flight near the Pentagon, the headquarters of the US Department of Defense (DoD) in Arlington County, Virginia.

ABOVE: **The Sikorsky HH-3F was given the name "Pelican" for its service in the US Coast Guard.**
RIGHT: **On May 6, 1994, the type was withdrawn from service, marking the end of USCG amphibious operations. Serial number 1430 was the first HH-3F to enter service with the USCG.**

The HH-3E was fitted with titanium protective armour and a defensive armament of three 7.62mm M60 machine-guns. The type was fitted with two external fuel tanks which could be jettisoned, self-sealing fuel tanks under the cabin floor and a high-speed rescue hoist. The HH-3E could accommodate 25 fully equipped troops or 15 stretchers and two attendants. The HH-3E was given the name "Jolly Green Giant" by crews operating the type in Vietnam.

The HH-3E was the first helicopter to be produced with a retractable fuel probe for air-to-air refuelling, and when fitted with external fuel tanks had a range limited only by the endurance of the crew. In 1967, to demonstrate the long-range capability of the type, two were flown non-stop from New York to the Paris Air Show, a distance of 6,872km/4,270 miles. This operation, during which each machine was air-to-air refuelled nine times, set a long-distance record for helicopters.

In 1967, the first aircraft of the type arrived in Vietnam, and were operated by the USAF from Udorn Air Base in

Thailand and Da Nang Air Base in South Vietnam. The long-range HH-3E enabled the USAF helicopters to conduct CSAR operations in Laos, Cambodia, South Vietnam and even North Vietnam. In 1970, US Army Special Forces were flown in an HH-3E Jolly Green Giant as part of a force which attempted the rescue of captured US personnel from a Prisoner of War (PoW) camp at Son Tay, located 37km/23 miles to the west of Hanoi, the capital of North Vietnam.

Twenty-five years later, during Operation Desert Storm (first Gulf War) in 1991, the HH-3E Jolly Green Giant was deployed to operate CSAR missions, during which 251 Coalition forces aircrew were rescued.

A licence was agreed between Sikorsky and Agusta to build the HH-3F in Italy as the AS-61R. In 1974,

production began, and 22 machines were built to replace Grumman HU-16 Albatross amphibious aircraft used in the SAR role by the Italian Air Force.

By 1995, all of the type in US service had been retired and replaced with the Sikorsky HH-60G Pave Hawk.

Sikorsky HH-3E

First flight: June 17, 1963
Power: 2 x General Electric T58-GE-10 turboshaft
Armament: 7.62mm M60 machine-gun
Size: Rotor diameter – 18.79m/62ft
Length overall – 22.15m/72ft 8in
Height – 5.46m/18ft 1in
Weights: Empty – 4,429kg/9,763lb
Take-off – 10,002 kg/22,050lb (maximum)
Performance: Speed – 262kph/164mph (maximum)
Service ceiling – 3,636m/12,000ft
Range – 965km/600 miles

Sikorsky CH-54 Tarhe

The S-60 prototype powered by two Pratt & Whitney R2800-54 radial piston engines (as used on the H-37 Mojave) was flown for first time on March 25, 1959. The machine crashed on April 3, 1961, but Sikorsky had already commenced development of the larger and more powerful S-64 which could lift an impressive 5,443kg/12,000lb payload. The first of six pre-production YCH-54As ordered by the US Army was flown on May 6, 1962. The machines were powered by two Pratt & Whitney T73-P-1 turboshaft engines driving a six-blade main rotor. Following a successful test-flying programme, the US Army placed an order for 54 of the production CH-54As. The West German armed forces evaluated the type but did not proceed with an order. The US Army then went on to order 37 of the heavier CH-54Bs fitted with the more powerful Pratt & Whitney T73-P-700 turboshaft engine, which had sufficient power to allow single-engine operations. Following a US Army tradition, the type was named "Tarhe" after a chief of the Wyandot, a Native American Indian tribe.

The CH-54 was an early example of modular design, as the power unit and even the cockpit section could be easily removed and fitted to another airframe in the field. A window across the rear wall of the cockpit allowed the co-pilot to operate the cargo winch and observe loading operations. Cargo could be handled in this manner with the helicopter held in the hover. The Universal Military Pod (UMP), a multi-purpose cargo container specifically designed to fit under the fuselage of a CH-54, could accommodate 87 fully equipped troops for helicopter assault operations. The UMP could also be configured as a combat command post or as a field hospital. Later, the UMP was fitted with a cargo hook to carry an under-slung load. On November 4, 1971, a CH-54B was flown to a world record altitude for helicopters of 11,010m/36,122ft.

The CH-54B was deployed around the world by the US Army, and in Vietnam the type was used operationally by the 478th and the 291st Aviation Companies to recover 380 downed US military aircraft.

ABOVE: **The Tarhe retained the rear-view window for the co-pilot first fitted in the S-60. On November 4, 1971, a CH-54B set the record for the highest level helicopter flight at 11,010m/36,122ft.**

The specialized BLU-82B Daisy Cutter, a 6,000kg/15,000lb bomb design to flatten an area of forest or scrub, was test dropped from a CH-54A Tarhe over Vietnam. The weapon was later dropped only from the Lockheed C-130 Hercules.

Budget cuts led to the cancellation of the Heavy Lift Helicopter (HLH) programme. Operations with the CH-54B Tarhe continued, but were supplemented by the Boeing CH-47 Chinook which eventually replaced the type in the heavy lift role.

The type had also been manufactured by the Sikorsky Aircraft Corporation for the civilian market as the S-64 Skycrane. Many ex-military machines were purchased by civilian operators. Erickson Air-Crane Inc. of Portland, Oregon, negotiated to buy the production rights and certification from the Sikorsky Aircraft Corporation, and continues to manufacture the type as

the Erickson S-64 Aircrane. The company also operates the largest fleet of S-64 helicopters in the world which are used to lift large loads. Machines in the Erickson fleet can be equipped with water-bombing equipment for firefighting operations.

The five-blade rotor, tail rotor and drive system from the CH-54B were used basically unchanged on the very successful Sikorsky S-65 (CH-53) series of helicopters. In 1958, the same equipment had been licensed by Westland Helicopters for use on the Westminster helicopter, of which only two prototypes were built. First flown on June 15, 1958, the type was eventually scrapped and the parts returned to Sikorsky.

ABOVE: **The Sikorsky CH-54 was an ingenious design – to save airframe weight and for ease of servicing, the engines, gearbox and drive to the tail rotor were left uncovered.** BELOW: **The Universal Military Pod (UMP) multi-purpose container was specifically designed for the CH-54. The UMP was used to transport troops or cargo, or could be equipped as a command post or a portable field hospital.**

Sikorsky CH-54B Tarhe

First flight: May 9, 1962
Power: 2 x Pratt & Whitney T73-P-700 turboshaft
Armament: None
Size: Rotor diameter – 21.95m/72ft
    Length – 26.97m/88ft 6in
    Height – 7.75m/25ft 5in
Weights: Empty – 8,981kg/19,800lb
    Take-off – 21,319kg/47,000lb (maximum)
Performance: Speed – 241kph/150mph (maximum)
    Service ceiling – 5,587m/18,330ft
    Range – 370km/230 miles

LEFT: **A US Marine Corps CH-53 Sea Stallion approaching the flight deck of the Nimitz-class aircraft carrier USS** *Harry S. Truman* **(CVN-75) for landing. Note the fixed refuelling probe in position on the nose of the aircraft.**

Sikorsky CH-53 Sea Stallion

In 1960, the US Navy began the process of identifying a replacement for the Sikorsky CH-37 Mojave in the heavy-lift role. In January 1961, a Tri-Service Assault Transport Program (TSATP) was proposed, and the type selected for development was the Vought-Hiller-Ryan XC-43, a four-engine tilt-wing experimental aircraft. The Bureau of Naval Weapons (BuWeps), acting on behalf of the USMC, initiated the Heavy Helicopter Experimental Program (HHXP). In August 1962, a decision was made to contract Sikorsky to develop the S-65A

as the YHC-53A. The type was first flown on October 14, 1966, at the Sikorsky airfield in Stratford, Connecticut. Deliveries of the production CH-53A to the USMC began in 1966.

Sikorsky decided to use the proven six-blade main rotor system, gearbox, transmission and tail rotor from the S-64 Skycrane/CH-54 Tarhe. The fuselage was of similar dimensions to that of the HH-3 and, although watertight, it was designed only for an emergency landing on water. A door was fitted in the starboard side and armour was fitted to crew areas and

to protect vital equipment. The mechanical flight controls were backed up by three hydraulic systems. On US Navy and USMC machines, the main rotor and tail boom were designed to fold for stowage on board a ship.

The first USMC squadron (HMH-463) to receive the type was deployed to Southeast Asia, and from mid-January 1967 operated a four aircraft detachment from a base near Da Nang, South Vietnam. On January 25, a CH-53A was deployed to recover a damaged Sikorsky UH-34 Choctaw from a ship and airlift the machine to a land base for repair. By the end of May, the four helicopters had been used to carry out over 100 successful recovery operations of 72 Sikorsky UH-34 Choctaws, 13 Piasecki CH-46 Sea Knights, 16 Bell UH-1E Iroquois and a number of fixed-wing aircraft. The fact that just four helicopters were able to

LEFT: **A Sikorsky CH-53G in service with the German Army. All the machines are being upgraded to allow the type to remain in front-line service for more years than originally planned.**

retrieve such a large number of valuable military assets in such a short period was proof of the wisdom of developing this very capable heavy-lift helicopter. On May 22, 1967, the rest of the squadron arrived and with a total of 26 helicopters on strength, the unit was called on to undertake a wider range of heavy-lift duties, including transporting up to 38 combat troops or moving heavy artillery weapons slung under the fuselage on a cargo hook.

Despite an impressive combat record, only some 150 of the CH-53A were built. The D model was fitted with the more powerful General Electric T64-GE-413 turboshaft engine, which allowed up to 55 fully equipped troops or a heavier cargo load to be transported. Delivery of the improved CH-53D began in March

1969. Compared to other types, the CH-53D had a relatively short production run, which ended in early 1972 after some 120 had been completed. Virtually all of these helicopters were deployed to the war in South-east Asia.

The USN operated the RH-53D, equipped with an air-to-air refuelling probe, for mine-countermeasures operations. Only the US Air Force operated the CH-53C for Special Forces missions and later as a cargo transport. The CH-53D was built for the (West) German army, and the first 20 were assembled from Sikorsky-supplied parts by VFW-Fokker. The German company Speyer then assembled a further 90 machines. In total, 112 were acquired (including two supplied by Sikorsky)

and were designated CH-53G. Versions of the CH-53D were also exported to Austria and sold on to Iran (RH-53D), Israel (S-65C-3) and Mexico (S-65C-3), which were purchased from Israel.

The Sikorsky CH-53D Sea Stallion was used extensively for seaborne and land-based operations, and was to remain the prime heavy-lift helicopter for the USMC until the Sikorsky CH-53E Super Stallion, an improved three-engine variant, entered service in 1981. The CH-53D continued to be used in front-line service to transport combat equipment and personnel, and was used extensively during Operation Desert Storm (first Gulf War) in 1991.

At the time of writing, the Israeli military was planning to keep the S-65C-3 Ya'sur in service until 2025. The USMC is expected to retire their last operational machines before 2018.

ABOVE: **A CH-53A Sea Stallion on a recently installed landing mat at a USMC fire support base positioned on the top of a mountain in South Vietnam.**

Sikorsky CH-53A Sea Stallion

First flight: October 14, 1964
Power: 2 x General Electric T64-6 turboshaft
Armament: 7.62mm M60 or 12.7mm machine-guns
Size: Rotor diameter – 22.02m/72ft 3in
Length (with rotors turning) – 26.9m/86ft 3in
Height – 7.6m/24ft 11in
Weights: Empty – 10,181kg/22,444lb
Take-off – 16,965kg/37,400lb (maximum)
Performance: Speed – 315kph/196mph (maximum)
Service ceiling – 6,401m/21,000ft
Range – 869km/540 miles

Sikorsky UH-60 Black Hawk

The Sikorsky UH-60 Black Hawk tactical assault helicopter is one of the most significant military helicopters ever to be produced. The type has been operational for over 30 years and continues in service with the US military and other forces around the world. In 1991, during Operation Desert Storm (first Gulf War), it was reported that over 1,000,000 troops were transported by Sikorsky UH-60 Black Hawk helicopters.

In 1972, the US Army initiated the Utility Tactical Transport Aircraft System (UTTAS) competition for find a replacement for the Bell UH-1 Iroquois. The design selected was the Sikorsky S-70. The prototype YUH-60A was first flown on October 17, 1974, and after extensive flight and development testing the type entered US Army service the 101st Airborne Division as the UH-60A in June 1979. Following a US Army tradition, the type was named "Black Hawk" after the Native American Indian tribe.

The UH-60A was flown by a crew of two pilots and two crewmen, and accommodated 11 fully equipped troops. Operating in battlefront conditions is dangerous, and during a mission a helicopter could easily sustain serious damage, sometimes enough to cause the aircraft to crash. With this is mind, Sikorsky built a number of survivability features into the machine. The rotor head and rotor blades were designed to take and survive direct machine-gun fire.

ABOVE: **A UH-60L Black Hawk helicopter flying a low-level mission over Iraq. The L model is a UH-60A with upgraded engines, stronger gearbox and an updated flight control system.**

Speed is vital when dropping troops (large cabin doors aid rapid egress), and the undercarriage was designed to take a vertical impact of up to 45kph/28mph. The engine exhausts are covered by infra-red suppressors to disguise the heat signature of exhaust gases and reduce the threat from a heat-seeking missile. The engines are mounted apart, again to reduce the risk of battle damage. The fuselage has a low-profile shape to reduce target area. The UH-60A Black Hawk can also carry a substantial cargo load internally or slung on cargo hooks mounted on the underside of the fuselage.

In 1987, the US Army ordered the improved UH-60L and included all the modifications and upgrades previously made to the UH-60A in service. The UH-60L was fitted with the more powerful General Electric T700-GE-701C engine, allowing the cargo lifting capacity to be increased by 454kg/1,000lb up to an impressive 4,100kg/9,000lb. This was a vital improvement as troops were equipped with more and heavier equipment. Sikorsky began production of the UH-60L Black Hawk in 1989.

Work on the further improved UH-60M began in 2001, with the intention of keeping the type as a front-line

ABOVE: **Two UH-60 Black Hawk helicopters taking off after delivering supplies and troops to the 155th Brigade Combat Team positioned at Forward Operating Base Hotel, near Najaf, Iraq.**

helicopter into the 2020s. The UH-60M was fitted with the upgraded General Electric T700-GE-701D engine. Other improvements included a strengthened cabin floor, impact absorbing crew seats, jettisonable cockpit doors and a wire strike protection system. An avionics upgrade included the fitting of a Global Positioning System (GPS) and an Automatic Direction Finder (ADF). For transportation or stowage on board a ship, the main and tail rotor blades, tail boom and stabilator are designed to be foldable. In July 2006, the first UH-60M Black Hawk was delivered to the US Army for evaluation, and this was followed by an order for 1,227 machines.

The Black Hawk can be fitted with stub wings on the upper fuselage to mount a range of additional weapons, including unguided rocket pods, anti-tank missiles or machine-gun pods. External fuel tanks can be carried, which substantially increase the operational range of the type.

The US Army first used the UH-60 in battle during Operation Urgent Fury, the invasion of Grenada, October 25, 1983,

RIGHT: **The UH-60Q operated by the US Army is a sophisticated air ambulance fitted to carry six casualties on stretchers. The type has an oxygen-generating system and other specialized emergency treatment equipment.**

and then for Operation Just Cause, the invasion of Panama, December 20, 1989. In 1991, during Operation Desert Storm, the US Army deployed some 300 of the type in the largest-ever air-assault operation. The UH-60 was used on the battlefield again during Operation Iraqi Freedom, the invasion of Iraq, in September, 2003. The type is currently being used in Afghanistan during the ongoing Operation Enduring Freedom. The UH-60 has also been used in action by US forces in Somalia, the Balkans and Haiti. Export customers include the Columbian National Police, Air Force

and Army, who use the helicopter in the war against drug operators and guerrilla forces. A gunship version has been developed for these operations. The Israeli military have used ex-US Army UH-60 Black Hawk helicopters for air operations against targets in Lebanon. The Mexican Air Force acquired the type for Special Forces operations against drug runners; the Federal Police and Mexican Navy also operate the type. The S-70i Black Hawk, an international military version, is assembled by PZL Mielec, a subsidiary of Sikorsky, in Poland.

LEFT AND ABOVE: **The tail rotor is angled at 20 degrees off the vertical. It creates thrust to allow for changes to the machine's centre of gravity as fuel is used and the aircraft becomes lighter. The automatic all-flying stabilator senses changes in airspeed and operates during the hover to keep the helicopter stable.**

Sikorsky UH-60A Black Hawk

First flight: October 17, 1974
Power: 2 x General Electric T700-GE-700 turboshaft
Armament: 7.62mm machine-gun
Size: Rotor diameter – 16.36m/53ft 8in
Length – 19.76m/64ft 10in
Height – 5.13m/16ft 10in
Weights: Empty – 4,819kg/10,624lb
Take-off – 9,185kg/20,250lb (maximum)
Performance: Speed – 296kph/184mph (maximum)
Ceiling – 5,700m/19,000ft
Range – 600km/370 miles

Sikorsky HH-60G Pave Hawk

Since 1987, the HH-60G Pave Hawk has been the prime rescue helicopter in United States Air Force service. The type is operated by many elements of the USAF, including Air Combat Command (ACC), Pacific Air Force (PAF), Air Education and Training Command (AETC), US Air Force Europe (USAFE), Air National Guard (ANG) and the Air Force Reserve Command (AFRC). During Operation Desert Storm, Pave Hawks provided combat search and rescue coverage for coalition forces in western Iraq, along the coast of Kuwait, the Persian Gulf and Saudi Arabia. The type was also deployed to execute emergency evacuation for US Navy SEAL combat teams inserted into Kuwait before the invasion was launched.

ABOVE: **The HH-60G Pave Hawk has an impressive performance, and is one of the few rescue helicopters equipped with an attack capability.**

The HH-60G Pave Hawk is primarily operated in the Combat Search and Rescue (CSAR) role to recover downed aircrew or any forces that have become isolated in enemy territory, day or night and in all weather conditions.

LEFT: **A rescue swimmer jumping from an HH-60J during a demonstration flight.** ABOVE: **The Sikorsky HH-60J Jayhawk is based on the SH-60 Seahawk helicopter, and replaced the HH-3F Pelican in US Coast Guard service.**

The HH-60G is a highly modified version of the UH-60 Black Hawk, and features an upgraded navigation suite that includes integrated Inertial Navigation System (INS), Global Positioning System (GPS) and Doppler navigation. The type is fitted with satellite, secure voice and Have Quick communications equipment. All HH-60G machines have an automatic flight control system, a Night Vision Goggles (NVG) facility and Forward Looking Infra-red (FLIR) sensors that allow the crew to fly the helicopter at low level on night operations. Additionally, the type is equipped with all-colour weather radar and an anti-icing system for the engine and main rotor blades, allowing the machine to be operated in all weather conditions.

Mission equipment includes a retractable inflight refuelling probe, internal auxiliary fuel tanks, two 7.62mm or 0.50in machine-guns, and a 3,600kg/8,000lb capacity cargo hook mounted under the fuselage. All are fitted with folding rotor blades for transportation (or stowage on board a ship), allowing a number to be carried in a Boeing C-17 Globemaster II or Lockheed C-5 Galaxy transport aircraft.

For improved survivability in combat conditions, all have a radar warning receiver, infra-red jammer and a flare/chaff countermeasures dispensing system. Rescue equipment includes a hoist with a lifting capacity of 272kg/600lb and a personnel locating system which provides range and bearing information, and is compatible with the PRC-112 survival radio.

During the Kosovo war, Pave Hawks provided continuous CSAR coverage for NATO air forces, and were successfully used to recover two USAF pilots shot down and isolated behind enemy lines.

In March 2000, three HH-60G Pave Hawk helicopters were deployed to Mozambique in support of an international flood relief operation, and in 17 days a total of 240 missions were flown to deliver more than 162,752kg/358,400lb of humanitarian supplies. After Hurricane Katrina in September 2005, more than 20 of the type from USAF Reserve (USAFR) and Air National Guard (ANG) units were deployed in support of recovery operations in New Orleans and surrounding areas. Pave Hawk crews flew operations around the

ABOVE: **Two Sikorsky HH-60G Pave Hawk helicopters during Angel Thunder, a Combat Search and Rescue (CSAR) exercise held at Davis-Monthan Air Force Base (AFB) in the Arizona Desert.**

clock for nearly a month, saving more than 2,900 civilians from the post-hurricane devastation.

The HH-60G was among the many different types of helicopter flown by the US military during Operation Iraqi Freedom in 2003. The type is currently in service on the battlegrounds of Afghanistan in support of coalition forces fighting in Operation Enduring Freedom.

Sikorsky HH-60G Pave Hawk

First flight: October 17, 1974
Power: 2 x General Electric T700-GE-700 turboshaft
Armament: 7.62mm or 0.50in machine-gun
Size: Rotor diameter – 14.1m/53ft 7in
Length – 17.1m/64ft 8in
Height – 4.4m/16ft 8in
Weights: Empty – 7,260kg/16,000lb
Take-off – 9,900kg/ 22,000lb (maximum)
Performance: Speed – 296kph/184mph (maximum)
Service ceiling – 4,627m/14,000ft
Range – 933km/580 miles

Sikorsky SH-60 Seahawk

The Seahawk is the standard anti-submarine helicopter operated from ships of the US Navy. In the late 1970s, the US Navy issued a requirement for an updated Light Airborne Multi-Purpose System (LAMPS) helicopter to operate from smaller naval escorts, and both Boeing and Sikorsky submitted design proposals. Following a fly-off, the Sikorsky machine, a development of the UH-60A Black Hawk, was named the winner. While the SH-60 used the same basic airframe and components of the UH-60A, the type was far more expensive and complex due to the fitting of extensive avionics equipment and weapons systems. The USN took delivery of the SH-60B Seahawk in 1983.

ABOVE: **An AGM-119 Penguin anti-shipping missile being launched from a Sikorsky SH-60 Seahawk. The Norwegian-built missile is designed to skim the surface at high speed, and has a range of 55km/34 miles.**

The SH-60 is designed to be operated day and night at sea and in all weather conditions. The primary mission for the type is to search for enemy submarines or surface vessels that may pose a threat. The SH-60B Seahawk is equipped for anti-submarine warfare with a complex system of sensors, including a towed Magnetic Anomaly Detector (MAD) and air-launched sonobuoys (from a Sikorsky-designed launcher). The SH-60B is also used for Anti-Shipping Surveillance and Targeting (ASST) to extend the defensive radar range, and is operated from aircraft carriers, cruisers, destroyers and frigates of the USN. The SH-60 has a range of 600km/373 miles and can remain on station for several hours. The internal fuel tanks hold 2,250 litres/ 496 gallons, but the machine can be fitted with an inflight refuelling system. However, this can only be used when the helicopter is held in the hover.

LEFT: **The Forward Looking Infra-Red (FLIR) turret is positioned on a mounting fitted to the nose of the SH-60 Seahawk. An ARN-146 positioning indicator forms part of the equipment.**

LEFT: **A US Marine Corps Seahawk hovering above the ground to evacuate a simulated casualty during an exercise.**

The SH-60B is operated by a pilot, a co-pilot/Airborne Tactical Officer (ATO) and an enlisted Aviation Systems Warfare Operator (ASWO). The type's roles include SAR, Vertical Replenishment (VertRep) at sea and MEDEVAC missions. In the VertRep role, the type can carry up to 1,800kg/ 3,968lb of internal cargo and up to 2,725kg/6,007lb on an external cargo hook.

The SH-60F is produced only for carrier-based ASW and SAR operations. The type differs from the SH-60B by being fitted with AQS-13F dipping sonar in place of MAD equipment, and is not armed with anti-shipping missiles. The SH-60F carries 14 sonobuoys rather than the 25 carried by an SH-60B. It is capable of carrying the Mk 46 ALT and an M-60D, M-240 or GAU-16 machine-gun mounted in the cabin door opening for defence.

Sensors and related equipment include an APS-124 search radar, UHF direction finding system, infra-red jammers and a radar altimeter. For defence, the SH-60 is equipped with a chaff/flare dispenser and missile warning sensors. Optional equipment includes a nose-mounted Forward Looking Infra-Red (FLIR) turret, and an ARN-146 position indicator to alert the sonar operator when the helicopter is directly over

a submerged submarine. The primary attack weapon is the Mk 46 or Mk 50 Advanced Lightweight Torpedo (ALT) and the AGM-114 Hellfire missile. For defence, an M-60D or GAU-16 machine-gun can be mounted in the cabin door space.

To deal with surface threats, the SH-60 carries the AGM-119B Penguin anti-shipping missile. Target acquisition is carried out using a thermal imaging unit fitted with a laser designator.

The Sikorsky SH-60 Seahawk has been exported and is operated by the navies of Australia, Brazil, Greece, Taiwan, Thailand, Turkey, Singapore and Spain. In Japan, Mitsubishi Heavy Industries are building the SH-60K under licence, fitted with more powerful engines and upgraded avionics, for the Japanese Maritime Self-Defense Force (JMSDF).

ABOVE: **An SH-60H Seahawk being used to transport ordnance from the Military Sealift Command ship USNS *Walter S. Diehl* (T-AO-193) to USS *Nimitz* (CVN-68) during a Vertical Replenishment.**

Sikorsky SH-60B Seahawk

First flight: December 12, 1979
Power: 2 x General Electric T700-401 turboshaft
Armament: AGM-84 Harpoon, AGM-114 Hellfire, AGM-119 Penguin, Sea Skua, Mk 46 or Mk 50 torpedo, Mk 36 mine, Mk 35 depth charge
Size: Rotor diameter – 16.36m/33ft 8in
 Length – 19.76m/64ft 10in
 Height – 5.18m/17ft 10in
Weights: Empty – 6,190kg/13,650lb
 Take-off – 9,925kg/ 21,884lb (maximum)
Performance: Speed – 235kph/145mph (maximum)
 Service ceiling – 5,790m/19,000ft
 Range – 600km/373 miles

Sikorsky MH-60G Pave Hawk

The United States Air Force describes the primary wartime mission for the MH-60G Pave Hawk as "the infiltration, extraction and resupply of Special Operations forces", which of course includes deployment of the type to rescue aircrew shot down over enemy territory.

In 1981, the USAF selected the Sikorsky UH-60 Black Hawk as a replacement for the Sikorsky HH-53E Jolly Green Giant and began an immediate programme to upgrade the type by fitting the PAVE electronics system, air-to-air refuelling probe and improved fuel capacity.

In December 1987, the more sophisticated UH-60A Credible Hawk entered service with the USAF 55th Aerospace Rescue and Recovery Squadron (ARRS) at Eglin Air Force Base (AFB), Florida. Later, all were upgraded to the same standard as new-build MH-60G machines.

ABOVE: **The airframe of the Sikorsky MH-60G Pave Hawk is designed to absorb battle damage. The main rotor blades are manufactured from titanium and composite materials, and can take direct hits from up to 23mm ammunition.**
LEFT: **A Sikorsky MH-60G Pave Hawk on a rescue training mission over the Nevada desert. For operations after dark, the flight crew are equipped with the Night Vision Goggles (NVG) facility and a Forward Looking Infra-Red (FLIR) system.**

The type could be transported in a large aircraft such as the Lockheed C-5A Galaxy (up to five MH-60Gs can be carried), Boeing C-17 Globemaster II or on a logistics transport ship. The blades of the main rotor were designed to fold back to reduce stowage space. A ground crew were able to prepare the helicopter for loading in less than an hour. Off-loading and re-assembly was achieved in less than two hours. The fuel system on the MH-60G allowed the type to be refuelled using a pressure or gravity feed system at Forward Area Arming and Refuelling Points (FAARP).

Avionics fitted in the MH-60G include terrain-following radar, voice altitude warning system and Forward Looking Infra-Red (FLIR) radar. With these, the crew can fly the machine in all weathers, day or night and at low level below enemy radar. The type is also equipped with Global Positioning System (GPS), an Inertial Navigation System (INS) and Doppler radar. The MH-60G is fitted with an automatic flight control system to stabilize the aircraft in flight. To operate over hostile airspace, the helicopter is fitted with an APR-39A(V)1 radar warning receiver, an ALQ-144A infra-red jammer

and an M130 chaff dispenser as defence against enemy radar and heat-seeking missiles. To locate downed aircrew, a range and bearing receiver compatible to the PRO-112 survival radio is fitted. A Hover Infra-red Suppressor System (HISS) is fitted to reduce the heat signature of the engine exhausts.

In 1991, during Operation Desert Storm, the USAF operated the type on Combat Search and Rescue (CSAR) missions, flying deep into enemy territory to locate and rescue any downed pilot. These missions were typically supported and defended by aircraft of the Coalition invasion force. The MH-60G was deployed by the USAF for CSAR duties in support of NATO forces engaged in Operation Allied Force, the large-scale bombing campaign to destroy the Yugoslav military infrastructure. During these operations, two USAF pilots were rescued from enemy territory.

The MH-60G can accommodate 12 fully equipped US Special Forces troops if internal auxiliary fuel tanks are not carried. When internal fuel tanks are fitted, this capacity is reduced to 10 troops. The rescue hoist fitted on the MH-60G has a 76m/250ft cable

ABOVE: **A Sikorsky MH-60G Pave Hawk landing during a Combat Search and Rescue (CSAR) mission. The type is equipped for day or night operations and in all weather conditions. The machine is fitted with a fixed air-to-air refuelling probe.**

and a lifting capacity of 272kg/600lb. If a landing to extract troops is impossible, Special Patrol Insertion-Extraction (SPIE) netting is hung from the helicopter to allow the troops to clip-on and be lifted to safety. An External Stores Support System (ESSS) is fitted under the fuselage to lift up to 3,629kg/8,000lb of supplies and equipment.

Sikorsky MH-60G Pave Hawk

First flight: October 17, 1974
Power: 2 x General Electric T700-GE-701C/D turboshaft
Armament: 0.50in GAU-18/A machine-gun
Size: Rotor diameter – 16.36m/53ft 8in
 Length – 17.1m/64ft 8in
 Height – 4.4m/16ft 8in
Weights: Empty – 6,400kg/14,109lb
 Take-off – 9,979kg/22,000lb (maximum)
Performance: Speed – 299kph/186mph (maximum)
 Ceiling – 4,267m/14,000ft
 Range – 716km/445 miles

Sikorsky CH-53E Super Stallion

In 1962, the US Marine Corps initiated the Heavy Helicopter Experimental (HHX) competition, which was won by the Sikorsky Aircraft Corporation with a three-engine development of the proven CH-53 Sea Stallion. The prototype XCH-53E was flown on March 1, 1974, and the first pre-production YHC-53E was flown on December 12, 1975. An initial order for 33 was placed by the USMC, followed by an order for 16 from the US Navy. The CH-53E Super Stallion entered service with the USMC on June 16, 1981.

The aircraft is powered by three General Electric T64-GE-416 turboshaft engines driving a seven-blade main rotor fabricated (as are the tail rotor blades) from a titanium and glass-fibre composite material. A total of 172 machines were built (the last in November 2003) and the majority deployed with USMC units in the Pacific and Atlantic Fleets. Those in USN service operate in the transport role.

The CH-53E is the largest and heaviest helicopter in service with US military forces. The type is operated for the transportation of troops and equipment during the initial assault phase of an amphibious operation, then to deliver reinforcements and supplies in subsequent operations. The CH-53E can be operated from ships by day or night, and in the most adverse weather conditions.

ABOVE: **A USMC Sikorsky CH-53E Super Stallion from HMH-461 Det. A flying over the Red Desert in Kandahar Province, Afghanistan.**

The helicopter is capable of lifting up to 16,257kg/35,840lb at sea level, and transporting the load over an operational radius of 93km/58 miles. A typical cargo would be a 7,258kg/16,000lb M198 howitzer, the gun's crew and ammunition, or an eight-wheeled Light Armoured Vehicle (LAV-25) weighing 11,794kg/26,000lb.

Flight instrumentation includes a four-axis autopilot, an auto-stabilized digital flight control system, an attitude and heading reference system, a Global Positioning System (GPS) and an AN/APN-217 Doppler radar.

RIGHT: **A CH-53E Super Stallion from Marine Heavy Helicopter Squadron 361 (MHM-361) high above the Pacific Ocean, on the way to perform a daytime tactics training exercise.**

RIGHT: **US Marines boarding a CH-53E Super Stallion helicopter on the amphibious assault ship USS *Bataan* (LHD-5) in the Persian Gulf. The helicopter is operated by Medium Marine Helicopter Squadron 264 (HMH-264).**

The cockpit is equipped with Pilot Night Vision System (PVNS) and Integrated Helmet and Display Sighting System (IHADSS) to allow the type to be flown on low-altitude operations at night or in adverse weather conditions.

The cabin can be configured in a number of ways and although it is fitted with 37 folding canvas seats along the sides as standard, the addition of a centre row increases the total capacity to 55. Up to seven standard cargo pallets can be accommodated, loaded through a door in the rear of the fuselage. A hydraulically operated rear ramp for the loading of freight is fitted. An external load lift system, developed by Skyhook Technologies Inc., mounted on the underside of the fuselage, allows loads of to up to 16,330kg/36,000lb to be carried.

The machine is equipped with a radar warning system and M130 chaff/flare dispensers as defence against heat-seeking missiles. The cowlings covering the engines and transmission are fabricated from a Kevlar laminate as protection against gunfire. The self-sealing fuel tanks are housed in the forward section on each side of the lower fuselage sponson. Further fuel can be carried in drop tanks which are mounted on each sponson. For long-range positioning flights, seven additional fuel tanks can be carried in the cabin. The CH-53E is also equipped with an air-to-air refuelling probe and is fitted with a hose-hoisting system to allow the aircraft to be refuelled from a surface ship without landing.

Armament comes in the form of a ramp-mounted weapon system developed and evaluated by the US Marine Corps. A 0.50in GAU-21/A reduced-recoil machine-gun, which can be installed and removed in less than two minutes, is "soft-mounted" on the cargo-loading ramp.

In January 1990, during Operation Eastern Exit, two Super Stallions carrying US Marines were flown from USS *Guam* (LPH-9) to rescue US and foreign nationals from the US Embassy in Mogadishu, the war-torn capital of Somalia. The mission was flown at night over a distance of 858km/533 miles, the helicopters being air-to-air refuelled twice en route. On June 8, 1995, two CH-53Es were deployed from USS *Keersage* (LHD-3) to rescue Capt. Scott O'Grady (USAF), an F-16 Fighting Falcon pilot who was shot down behind enemy lines in the province of Bosnia, Yugoslavia.

ABOVE: **Two CH-53E Super Stallion helicopters carrying cargo in nets being refuelled from a Lockheed C-130 Hercules during a long-range supply operation.**

Sikorsky CH-53E Super Stallion

First flight: March 1, 1974

Power: 3 x General Electric T64-GE-416 turboshaft

Armament: 0.50in GAU-21/A machine-gun

Size: Rotor diameter – 24.08m/79ft
Length – 20.19m/99ft 1in
Height – 8.97m/29ft 5in

Weights: Empty – 15,071kg/33,226lb
Take-off – 33,340kg/73,500lb (maximum)

Performance: Speed – 315kph/196mph (maximum)
Service ceiling – 5,634m/18,500ft
Range – 925km/574 miles

Sikorsky MH-53J Pave Low

The US Air Force used the MH-53 to penetrate enemy territory for special operations and aircrew recovery for more than 40 years. Capable of operating day or night or in bad weather, these large two-engine helicopters were used to conduct long-range, low-level missions to insert, extract and resupply US Special Operations Forces around the world.

The MH-53 helicopters were originally HH-53 helicopters used by the US Air Force in the Vietnam War which, over decades of service, received many upgrades and improvements. After the 1960s, all were essentially remanufactured, with the airframe being completely reskinned and the engines and rotor systems replaced. Along with the new lease of life came a new designation – MH-53 (M – Multi-mission and H – Helicopter).

The most significant enhancement to the helicopter was the Pave Low electronics programme which modified the type for operating at night and during bad weather. Equipped with Forward Looking Infra-Red (FLIR) sensors, Global Positioning System, Inertial Navigation System (INS) and terrain-following radar, the MH-53 could be flown on clandestine, low-level missions in all weathers, day or night, anywhere in the world. Folding rotor blades made the MH-53 aircraft carrier-compatible. If a clearing was not available when operating in jungle conditions, a device known as a Forest Penetrator, a type of heavy folding seat, could be lowered through the tree canopy to facilitate the rescue.

In the late 1980s, the USAF launched the Pave Low III programme, in which nine MH-53Hs and 32 HH-53s were modified for night and adverse weather operations. During the programme, the following items were improved or fitted: AN/AAQ-29A FLIR radar, GPS, INS, terrain-following radar and other integrated avionics to enable the crew

ABOVE: **A Sikorsky MH-53J Pave Low III on a training flight. The machine is from the US Air Force 20th Special Operations Squadron based at Hurlburt Field, Florida. The Pave Low III programme to modify HH-53 and MH-53 helicopters for night and all-weather operations began in the late 1980s.**

to navigate precisely to and from a target area. The USAF designated these modified aircraft as the MH-53J, the largest and heaviest helicopters in the USAF inventory and the most technologically advanced in the world.

The MH-53 carried a crew of six, consisting of two pilots, two flight engineers and two gunners manning a combination of 7.62mm Minigun or 0.50in M218 machine-guns. In the transport role, 38 fully equipped troops or 14 stretchers could be carried. An external cargo hook with a lifting capacity of 9,072kg/20,000lb was mounted under the fuselage.

In 1990, during Operation Desert Storm, MH-53s of the USAF provided the lead for US Army AH-64 Apaches during airstrikes on Iraqi defences to destroy the early warning radar system at the start of the bombing campaign. Infiltration, exfiltration and resupply missions for US Special Forces went on throughout the war. The type was also deployed in Iraq, Saudi Arabia, Kuwait and the Persian Gulf, to provide Search and Rescue coverage for the air forces of the Coalition. In 2003, the MH-53 was once again deployed to Iraq to support US Special Forces missions during Operation Lasting Freedom.

The MH-53M Pave Low IV system gave the aircrew instant access to the total battlefield situation on a colour digital map screen compatible with Night Vision Goggles. Using signals from satellite links,

ABOVE: **A Sikorsky MH-53J Pave Low III being prepared for the last operational flight of the type at an airfield in Iraq. All MH-53 helicopters were retired from US Air Force service on September 30, 2008.**

the system displayed virtually real-time information to identify potential hazards along the flight route or enemy radar.

In 2008, the US Air Force Special Operations Command (AFSOC) decided to retire the MH-53 from service, as it was no longer economically viable to keep the aircraft maintained in combat-ready condition. The type was replaced in service by the Bell Boeing CV-22B Osprey.

ABOVE: **A Sikorsky MH-53M Pave Low IV being refuelled from a Lockheed MH-130P Combat King aircraft during a training exercise. All MH-53 helicopters have been replaced in US Air Force service by the V-22 Osprey. Note the large rigid refuelling probe.**

Sikorsky MH-53J Pave Low

First flight: October 15, 1964
Power: 2 x General Electric T64-GE-7A turboshaft
Armament: 7.62mm Minigun or 0.50in M218 machine-gun
Size: Rotor diameter – 22.02m/72ft
  Length overall – 28m/88ft
  Height – 5.22m/17ft 2in
Weights: Empty – 10,691kg/23,570lb
  Take-off – 19,051kg/42,000lb (maximum)
Performance: Speed – 315kph/196mph (maximum)
  Service ceiling – 4,900m/16,000ft
  Range – 868km/540 miles

Sikorsky MH-53E Sea Dragon

The MH-53E Sea Dragon is a version of the CH-53E developed for the US Navy for the Airborne Mine Countermeasures (AMCM) role, with a secondary mission of shipboard delivery. The AMCM mission includes minesweeping, floating mine destruction, channel marking and towing of small surface craft. Operating from aircraft carriers and other warships, the MH-53E Sea Dragon can carry up to 55 fully equipped troops or a 16,257kg/35,840lb payload over a distance of 93km/58 miles, or a 10,161kg/22,400lb payload over 926km/580 miles. Additional capabilities include SAR, air-to-air refuelling and refuelling at the hover. The machine is fitted with an external cargo hook for Vertical Replenishment (VertRep) operations.

The prototype MH-53E was first flown on December 23, 1981. The first of some 50 deliveries to the USN began in 1986, and the type entered front-line service in April 1987. The MH-53E is heavier and has a greater fuel capacity than the CH-53E (12,112 litres/3,200 gallons), which is carried in larger sponsons each of which is fitted with two fuel tanks.

RIGHT: **A post-tsunami humanitarian mission in Indonesia. Civilians and crew are unloading food, clothing and relief supplies from the rear cargo ramp of an MH-53E Sea Dragon of Helicopter Mine Countermeasures Squadron 15 (HM-15).**

Although the Sea Dragon retains some 80 per cent commonality with the CH-53, it differs from the earlier version by being fitted with rear escape hatches, an improved tail rotor system and airframe structural reinforcement.

The MH-53E Sea Dragon can be used to deploy a formidable range of AMCM equipment. The aircraft is flown above the surface of a waterway, towing electronic or magnetic equipment to locate and clear mines. The main type of sweep used is the hydrofoil sled. This equipment (too large to be carried in the helicopter), which is towed at a relatively high speed across the water, is capable of detonating both acoustic and magnetic mines.

ABOVE: **A rainbow is formed in the ocean mist as a Helicopter Mine Countermeasures Squadron 15 (HM-15) Sikorsky MH-53E Sea Dragon conducts mine-countermeasures operations.**

The MH-53E can also operate the AN/SPU-1/W, a single magnetized orange pipe minesweeping system towed as a single unit or three units in tandem to detonate mines by magnetic influence. In contrast, the purely mechanical Mk-103 system is used for sweeping moored mines. This system is a wire-type sweep trailed from the helicopter and fitted with cutters to slice through mooring cables so that the submerged mines float to the surface to be neutralized.

The Airborne Laser Mine Detection System (ALMDS) is an airborne electro-optical system that is capable of rapid detection and classification of floating and moored mines located in relatively shallow water. With input from GPS, accurate navigation data is provided to determine target location. Using these systems can enable significant areas of sea to be rendered safe for friendly shipping. Perhaps these capabilities are best illustrated by the statistic from Operation Desert Storm in 1991, that one USN squadron

ABOVE: **Preparing to launch MK-103 minesweeping equipment from the rear ramp of an MH-53E Sea Dragon helicopter over the Persian Gulf.** RIGHT: **An MH-53E Sea Dragon towing a Mark 105 hydrofoil minesweeping sled while conducting simulated mine clearance operations.**

operating the MH-53E cleared over 1,000 Iraqi mines. For AMCM missions, the MH-53E is operated by a crew of seven: pilot, co-pilot, safety observer, two AMCM equipment handlers and two ramp operators.

In the cockpit, the pilots are assisted by a dual-digital automatic flight control system controlled by two computers that continually cross-check one another and disable any potential false inputs. If one computer fails, the other automatically doubles output, eliminating any degradation in automatic flight control performance.

The MH-53E was also procured by Japan directly from Sikorsky, and this version is designated S-80M-1 by the manufacturer.

ABOVE: **A Sikorsky MH-53E of Helicopter Mine Countermeasures Squadron 15 preparing to launch from the amphibious assault ship USS *Nassau* (LHA-4). The Sea Dragon is fitted with AN/ALE-39 Countermeasures Dispensing System (CDS), which can be mounted internally or externally and is designed to dispense chaff, infra-red decoy flares or expendable jammers.**

Sikorsky MH-53E Sea Dragon

First flight: December 23, 1981
Power: 3 x General Electric T64-GE-419 turboshaft
Armament: 0.50in M218 machine-gun
Size: Rotor diameter – 24.08m/79ft
  Length – 30.19m/99ft 1in
  Height – 8.6m/28ft 4in
Weights: Empty – 16,667kg/36,745lb
  Take-off – 31,616kg/69,700lb (maximum)
Performance: Speed – 278kph/173mph (maximum)
  Service ceiling – 3,048m/10,000ft
  Range – 1,931km/1,200 miles

Sikorsky Superhawk/CH-148 Cyclone

The Sikorsky H-92 was developed for military operation in parallel with the successful civil S-92 helicopter. The type has an airframe that incorporates some of the best design elements from the successful and proven Black Hawk, Seahawk and CH-53 series of military helicopters. The H-92 was first flown on December 23, 1998.

The H-92 can transport 22 fully equipped troops, or perform lift operations using the cargo hook with a lifting capacity of 4,536kg/ 10,000lb. The exceptionally large cabin offers a range of interior options to maximize flexibility, and it can accommodate vehicles or palletized stores up to a total weight of 4,421kg/9,748lb. The inbuilt cargo handling system has a 1,814kg/4,000lb capacity cargo winch and a floor-roller system to ease the loading and unloading of bulky items. A rear ramp allows easy and rapid loading and unloading of cargo and troops. Six stretcher cases plus medical attendants can be accommodated.

The airframe of the helicopter has been purposely designed for strength and enhanced extreme mission endurance. The H-92 has also been designed to be transportable in Lockheed C-5A Galaxy or Boeing C-17 Globemaster II transport aircraft, and takes less than two hours to prepare, load and deploy. Advanced military avionics include a Night Vision Goggles (NVG) compatible cockpit and Head-Up Display (HUD); and aircraft

ABOVE: **Safety features on the Sikorsky H-92 Superhawk include a high-visibility cockpit, crashworthy passenger seats and high energy-absorbing landing gear.**

survivability systems include designed-in crashworthiness and ballistic tolerance to direct hits from small arms.

RIGHT: **The H-92 is a military development of the civilian S-92. A number of government operators around the world have acquired versions for transport or military duties.**

RIGHT: **The H-92 is a large helicopter capable of accommodating 22 troops or freight internally, while having the capability to lift 4,536kg/10,000lb as an underslung load.**

The Canadian government selected the H-92 to satisfy a unique and challenging naval requirement. In November 2004, Canada's Department of National Defence (DoND) awarded a contract for 28 aircraft to the Sikorsky Aircraft Corporation. In Canadian service the aircraft is designated the CH-148 Cyclone, and it is replacing the Westland CH-124 Sea King, which has been in operation since the early 1960s. The first production CH-148 Cyclone was flown on November 15, 2008.

The CH-148 Cyclone, a dedicated naval version, is an extremely capable machine developed for maritime surveillance, reconnaissance, anti-submarine and anti-shipping operations. For stowage on board a ship, the type is fitted with a folding tail boom and folding main rotor blades. Self-sealing fuel tanks with a capacity of 3,030kg/6,680lb are fitted, as is an air-to-air refuelling probe. The type is also fitted with emergency flotation systems positioned under the fuselage and in the tail boom; these automatically inflate and are expected to keep the helicopter afloat and upright in up to Sea State 5 conditions. In addition, a 15-man life raft is installed in each sponson. The Cyclone has a metal and composite airframe, and a number of safety features such as engine burst containment have been incorporated into the design.

Concerns with the overall weight of the aircraft has led Sikorsky to consider an engine upgrade, but deliveries of aircraft (all to be modified later to the contracted specification) began in February 2010 at Canadian Forces Base (CFB), Shearwater. Sea trials on board HMCS *Montréal* began in March 2010, and all 28 of the type went into service in 2014.

BELOW: **Canada operates the CH-148 Cyclone, the military version of the type, for maritime duties. Equipped with active and passive sensors, the CH-148 is armed with ASW torpedoes.**

Sikorsky Superhawk

First flight: December 23, 1998
Power: 2 x General Electric CT7-8A7 turboshaft
Armament: 7.62mm C6 machine-gun
Size: Rotor diameter – 17.12m/56ft 2in
Length – 20.88m/68ft 6in
Height – 4.71m/15ft 5in
Weights: Empty – 7,359kg/16,223lb
Take-off – 12,837kg/28,300lb (maximum)
Performance: Speed – 306kph/190mph (maximum)
Service ceiling – 4,572m/15,000ft
Range – 1,521km/945 miles

LEFT: **The Sud-Ouest S.O.1221 Djinn has a skid-type undercarriage fitted with small retractable wheels to facilitate ground handling. The Djinn was the world's first production helicopter to make use of the cold jet principle of propulsion.**

Sud-Ouest S.O. 1221 Djinn

On May 14, 1947, two years after the end of World War II, the French company Sud-Ouest test-flew the S.O.1100 Ariel, built with the benefit of research carried out in Nazi Germany. The machine differed from most other designs in that the single three-blade rotor was powered by tipjets.

A Mathis G7 petrol engine drove a compressor to provide low-pressure air which was then fed through ducting inside each rotor blade to the combustion chamber in each tip-mounted pulse jet, where it was mixed with fuel and electrically ignited. The thrust generated powered the rotor.

Experience gained from the various versions of this experimental machine led to the development of the S.O.1220, which was first flown on January 2, 1953.

BELOW: **High-pressure air for the rotor tipjets was bled from the compressor of the Turboméca Palouste IV turbine engine.**

ABOVE: **The torqueless propulsion system did not require the machine to be fitted with a tail rotor.**

SUD-OUEST S.O. 1221 DJINN

RIGHT: **Twin fins and a central rudder provided added directional control, and the boom was left uncovered, which also saved weight.**

This led to the production of the S.O. 1221 Djinn (genie), but the crucial difference was that the rotor blades now had cold-jet propulsion, compressed air ducted from the compressor section of the Turboméca Palouste and blown from tip-mounted pods. The rotor was torqueless, and a tail rotor was not required to be fitted to the machine. Additionally, warm air ducted through the rotor blades was enough to provide de-icing.

The S.O.1220 was used to prove the viability of the propulsion system, and Sud-Ouest used this experience to help them build five prototypes of the S.O. 1221, the first being flown on December 16, 1953. Within days, a prototype machine set an altitude record for light helicopters of 4,789m/15,712ft.

The Djinn had the appearance of a conventional helicopter, with a two-seat side-by-side cockpit enclosed by a bubble-type canopy and transparent side doors. The Turboméca Palouste gas turbine engine (originally designed as an air generator and primarily used as an engine ground starter unit) was mounted behind the cockpit bulkhead to provide forward thrust and compressed air for the tip-mounted pods on the rotor blades. No tail rotor was fitted but the short tail boom, fabricated from welded steel tubing, was fitted with two vertical fins. A centrally mounted rudder, positioned in line with the engine exhaust, provided directional control. To save weight, the tail structure was uncovered.

The French Army was very interested by the highly manoeuvrable machine, and 22 pre-production airframes were built for evaluation, followed by an order for 100 machines. The US Army became interested in the Djinn because of the type's size, excellent manoeuvrability, ease of maintenance and relatively low unit cost. Three of the pre-production machines were sent to the US Army for

evaluation (serial numbers 57-6104 to 6106) and the experimental aircraft was designated YHO-1. No orders were placed by the US Army, apparently due to both budgetary and political constraints. A further six examples were purchased for the West German Army. In French military use, the Djinn was used for liaison, observation, CASEVAC (fitted with two removable stretcher carriers) and pilot training. A Djinn was used by the French Army for firing trials with the Nord SS10 anti-tank missile.

When production ended in the mid-1960s, a total of 178 of the type, including pre-production machines, had been built. When the type was retired from military use, many were registered with civilian operators and converted

for agricultural use by being fitted with aerial spraying equipment.

The Djinn was replaced in French military service by the Aérospatiale Alouette series of helicopters.

Sud-Ouest S.O. 1221 Djinn

First flight: December 16, 1953
Power: 1 x Turboméca Palouste IV gas turbine
Armament: None
Size: Rotor diameter – 11m/36ft 1in
Length – 5.3m/17ft 5in (fuselage)
Height – 2.6m/8ft 6in
Weights: Empty – 360kg/794lb
Take-off – 800kg/1,764lb (maximum)
Performance: Speed – 130kph/81mph (maximum)
Service ceiling – 1,463m/4,800ft
Range – 293km/180 miles

Westland Whirlwind

After World War II, service planners in the UK began to truly appreciate the potential of the helicopter as a military asset. However, design and development of the helicopter did not receive sufficient funding or production priority during the war years. Instead, the simplest way for the country to acquire a UK-produced helicopter was to build US-designed machines. Westland Aircraft Limited Helicopters of Yeovil negotiated with the Sikorsky Aircraft Corporation and agreed a licence to build the S-55 helicopter. The first aircraft to enter service with the Royal Navy were in fact built in the USA by Sikorsky and supplied under the Mutual Defense Assistance (MDA) programme. A total of 32 Sikorsky-built machines, powered by the Pratt & Whitney R01340-40 radial piston engine, were successfully trialled operationally by the Royal Navy.

The first Westland-built machine, powered by the Pratt & Whitney R-1340-40, was flown on August 15, 1953. The HAR.1, now named

RIGHT: **The Westland Whirlwind HAR.10 was fitted with the Rolls-Royce Gnome turboshaft engine. The engine was lighter and easier to maintain than a radial piston engine, and also gave an improvement in aircraft performance.**

Whirlwind, was delivered to the RN for use in the Air Sea Rescue (ASR) role. The almost identical HAR.2 was produced for the Royal Air Force and was deployed in the same role. The machines in RAF service were initially operated by RAF Coastal Command to provide ASR coverage for most of the UK. In reality, however, many rescue operations involved the recovery of civilians in dangerous situations.

ABOVE: **Only two Westland Whirlwind HCC Mk12s powered by a Rolls-Royce Gnome turboshaft engine were built. Both were assigned to the Royal Flight, and were later replaced for these duties by the Westland Wessex.**

The HAR.3 delivered to the RN was powered by the Wright R-1300-3 Cyclone 7 radial piston engine. The HAR.4 built for the RAF was equipped to operate in a hot climate and at higher altitudes, and all 24 built retained the

RIGHT: **The Westland Whirlwind HAR.3 delivered to the Royal Navy was powered by the Wright R-1300-3 Cyclone 7 radial piston engine. This was later changed to a Pratt & Whitney R-1340-57 for the HAR.4. The HAR.5 was powered by a British-built Alvis Leonides Major radial piston engine.**

Pratt & Whitney R-1340-57 engine. The HAR.4 first entered RAF service with No. 155 Squadron in September 1954, and operated transport and rescue missions in jungle conditions during the Malayan Emergency (1948–60). A number of HAR.4s were operated by the RAF in support of the British nuclear weapon testing programme from the base on Christmas Island in the Indian Ocean.

In 1955, the HAR.5 was fitted with the more powerful British-built Alvis Leonides Major radial piston engine, which gave the Whirlwind an improvement in overall performance.

BELOW: **The Whirlwind HAR Mk1 was powered by a Bristol-Siddeley (later Rolls-Royce) Gnome turboshaft engine, which gave the machine an improvement in performance and range.**

The HAR.5 was delivered to the British military and was exported to Austria.

The HAS.7, purposely built for the anti-submarine warfare role, was first flown on October 17, 1956, and entered service with No.845 Naval Air Squadron (NAS) in August 1957. The HAS.7 replaced the fixed-wing Fairey Gannet AS4 in the vital carrier-borne anti-submarine role. This version was equipped with radar and dipping ASDIC for detecting submarines, and could carry homing torpedoes. As the first British helicopter deployed in the role, this aircraft pioneered rotary wing ASW capability for the RN at a vital stage in the Cold War. Fleet Air Arm (FAA) squadrons operating the Whirlwind included No.814, 815, 820, 824, 845, 847 and 848 NAS, as well as No.705 and 771 Training Squadrons. Later, some were converted

for use in the ASR role and fitted with the much lighter and more powerful Bristol-Siddeley Gnome turboshaft engine; these were designated HAR.9.

In 1962, all HAR.2 and HAR.4 machines in RAF service were replaced by the Rolls-Royce Gnome-powered HAR.10. The first Gnome-powered Whirlwind had been flown in 1959, and can be most easily identified by the longer nose section. The HAR.10 was widely used by the RAF as a short-range tactical transport and training helicopter both in the UK and overseas, including operations over Borneo in late 1963. This version of the Whirlwind was also used extensively in supporting the British Army in Malaya, and could be equipped with four anti-tank missiles. The RAF continued to use the type in Cyprus for SAR duties until 1982.

Westland-built Whirlwinds were exported to Austria, Canada, Ghana, France, Jordan, Spain and Yugoslavia.

Westland Whirlwind HAR.3

First flight: August 15, 1953
Power: 1 x Wright R-1300-3 Cyclone 7 radial piston engine
Armament: None
Size: Rotor diameter – 16.15m/53ft
    Length – 12.88m/42ft 3in
    Height – 4.06m/13ft 4in
Weights: Empty – 2,381kg/5,250lb
    Take-off – 3,583kg/7,900lb (maximum)
Performance: Speed – 180kph/112mph (maximum)
    Service ceiling – 4,816m/15,800ft
    Range – 579km/360 miles

Westland Wessex

In 1955, a year after the Sikorsky S-58 Choctaw had been first flown, the Royal Navy issued a requirement for a turbine-powered helicopter equipped for anti-submarine warfare. Westland Aircraft Limited proposed a licence-built version of the S-58 already in service with the US Navy as the HSS-1 for the basis, but converted to be powered by a Napier Gazelle NGa.1 turboshaft engine. A Sikorsky-built HSS-1 was delivered to the Westland factory at Yeovil as a pattern airframe. To accommodate the longer turboshaft engine, the nose section of the aircraft had to be completely redesigned.

The first Westland-built machine was flown at Yeovil on May 17, 1957, and the first pre-production Wessex HAS.1 was flown on June 20, 1958. The first machines for the RN were delivered in April 1961. The Wessex entered Fleet Air Arm (FAA) squadron service with No.815 Naval Air Squadron (NAS) at Culdrose (HMS *Seahawk*) in July 1961.

RIGHT: **The Wessex was a considerable improvement on the original Sikorsky S-58 design. Note the starboard turbine exhaust below the cockpit.**

A total of 11 FAA squadrons were equipped with the HAS.1, the first purpose-designed ASW helicopter to be operated by the Fleet Air Arm. The only offensive weapons carried by this version were torpedoes.

The Wessex was also ordered by the Royal Air Force as the HC.2 for use as a troop transport. Seventy-four were built, and a number were later converted to HAR.2 for standard SAR duties. These also differed from the

ABOVE: **The Wessex served the British Armed Forces for three decades, seeing action with both the Royal Air Force and the Royal Navy.**

Wessex helicopters in FAA service by being powered by two Bristol Siddeley (later Rolls-Royce) Gnome Mk.110/111 turboshaft engines coupled to a common gearbox. The HC.2 could accommodate 16 fully equipped troops or lift a 1,814kg/4,000lb load in a cargo sling. The Gnome-powered versions

LEFT: **This side view of two Wessex helicopters in formation shows how different the nose of the British version was from the US version.**

are easily identifiable by a large single engine exhaust on each side of the nose. A version of the HC.2, the HU.5, was ordered as a troop transport for the Royal Marines, the first was delivered in December 1963, just six months after the prototype had been flown. For operating at sea and in the event of an emergency water landing, the HU.5 was equipped with rapid-inflation flotation bags stowed in housings mounted on the hub of each main undercarriage wheel. The HU.5 was flown by six RAF squadrons until 1987, and they were used on operations in Borneo, Oman and the Falkland Islands.

The Napier Gazelle-powered HAS.3 entered FAA service in January 1967. This version was equipped with improved radar equipment, and was fitted to carry torpedoes, depth charges and wire-guided missiles. A large radome for the search radar scanner was positioned on top of the fuselage. Inevitably, this version became known to FAA personnel as the Camel. Apart from three development aircraft, all were converted or, more accurately, rebuilt HAS.1 machines. Although the HAS.3 was planned to be withdrawn from service in early 1982, the type remained in squadron service until

December 1982, having been required for ASW operations in the Falklands War.

The destroyer HMS *Antrim* (D18) reached the South Atlantic before the main British task force arrived in April 1982. On April 22, an HAS.3 (XP142) operating from the ship was deployed to rescue a Special Air Service (SAS) reconnaissance party from a glacier after their transport (two Wessex HU.5s) had crashed in blizzard conditions. On April 25, the same machine flown by Lt Cmdr I. Stanley was deployed to attack and depth-charge the Argentine submarine *Santa Fe*. Although the helicopter was subsequently damaged by enemy small arms fire and bomb splinters, this machine survived and is now preserved by the Fleet Air Arm Museum, Yeovilton.

LEFT: **In Royal Navy service, the Wessex was operated in the transport, air sea rescue and anti-submarine warfare roles. In 1982, the type was deployed in action during the Falklands War.**

Westland Wessex HAS.2

First flight: May 17, 1958
Power: 1 x Napier Gazelle NGa.1 turboshaft
Armament: None
Size: Rotor diameter – 17.07m/56ft
    Length – 27.07m/65ft 10in
    Height – 4.85m/15ft 11in
Weights: Empty – 3,583kg/7,900lb
    Take-off – 6,169kg/13,600lb (maximum)
Performance: Speed – 212kph/132mph (maximum)
    Service ceiling – 3,048m/10,000ft
    Range – 628km/390 miles

LEFT: **Although originally developed for the Egyptian Air Force, the Westland Commando HC.4 is operated by the Royal Navy, and has become a key asset for amphibious operations by the Royal Marines.**

Westland Sea King

The Sea King manufactured by Westland Helicopters is a licence-built version of the Sikorsky S-61 helicopter, which is also known as the Sea King. Although these aircraft share a name, the British-built one differs considerably from the S-61 by being equipped with many British-built systems and components, including Rolls-Royce Gnome turboshaft engines, anti-submarine warfare systems and an automatic flight control system. The Westland Sea King was also developed for a much wider range of missions than the S-61s produced by Sikorsky.

A 1969 licence agreement between Westland and Sikorsky allowed the British company to use the Sea King airframe and rotor system as the basis for a machine to meet a Royal Navy requirement for a replacement for the Westland Wessex HAS.3 helicopter.

The prototype and three pre-production machines (SH-3D) were built by Sikorsky and delivered by sea in October 1966. Two pre-production development machines were used for trials and evaluation by Westland and subsequently by the Aeroplane and Armaments Experimental Establishment

(AAEE). The first Westland-built Sea King HAS.1 was flown on May 7, 1969, at Yeovil. In August 1969, the machine was delivered to No.700S Naval Air Squadron (NAS) Intensive Flight Trials Unit (IFTU), and was the first of 60 ordered by the RN. The last Westland Sea King to be built left the production line in 1990.

The basic ASW Sea King was upgraded a number of times as the HAS.2, HAS.5 and the HAS.6, which were replaced in service by the AgustaWestland Merlin MH1. A number of HAS.6 machines had the ASW equipment removed for the aircraft to be used in the transport role as part of the Commando Helicopter Force (CHF).

The Sea King HAR.3 developed for the RAF entered service from September 1977 to replace the Westland Whirlwind and, later, the Wessex, in the search and rescue role. These aircraft provide 24-hour emergency coverage around the UK and the Falkland Islands. SAR versions of the Sea King were also produced for the Royal Norwegian Air Force (RNAF), German Navy and later for the Belgian Air Force.

In 2003, during Operation Iraqi Freedom, a number of Sea King HC.4s were deployed from HMS *Ocean* (L12) to land the leading elements of the invasion force on the Al-Faw Peninsula. On return

LEFT: **Royal Navy HC.4 Sea Kings were flown repeatedly in support of the NATO (IFOR) presence in Bosnia, moving military equipment and undertaking many life-saving CASEVAC flights.**

LEFT: **To fulfil an urgent requirement for an Airborne Early Warning (AEW) aircraft, two machines were converted for this role as the Westland Sea King AEW.2A. The latest ASaC7 version is equipped with Thales 2000 Searchwater AEW radar, which provides accurate detection of air and ground targets.**

from operations in Iraq, all Sea King HC.4 helicopters needed to be upgraded to enable the type to be operated in the hot and high conditions found in Afghanistan. This included fitting an improved design of main rotor blade, a high-performance tail rotor and an updated Defensive Aids Suite (DAS). An improved type of Display Night Vision Goggles (DNVG) system was also fitted as part of the upgrade. This package of modifications resulted in the aircraft being redesignated as the Sea King Mk4+.

A troop-carrying version, the Commando, was originally developed for the Egyptian Air Force. Capable of transporting 27 fully equipped troops over 644km/400 miles, the type retained the foldable rotor blades and tail boom fitted to the naval variants. The Commando is fitted with an external cargo hook with a load-carrying capacity of up to 2,722kg/6,000lb. A rescue hoist is fitted as standard. In RN service, the type is designated Sea King HC.4 and remains in service as an important asset in the amphibious assault force. The aircraft is fitted with a Defensive Aids Suite (DAS) which offers a high standard of protection from both infra-red and radar-guided anti-aircraft weapons. It is equipped with a cabin-mounted 7.62mm General Purpose Machine Gun (GPMG) for defence and limited fire support.

During the Falklands War a number of RN warships, Royal Fleet Auxiliary (RFA) and transport ships were lost due to the lack of AEW coverage. In 1982, two Sea King HAS.2 helicopters were hastily modified to become the Sea King AEW.2A, and a total of 13 were eventually completed. The AEW.2A was fitted with the Thorn-EMI ARI-5930/3 Searchwater radar, the scanner for which was mounted on a swivelling arm attached to the side of the fuselage and protected by an inflatable dome. The radar scanner is lowered in flight and raised before landing. A further upgrade of the AEW.7 included fitting Thales 2000 Searchwater radar and LINK16 data link equipment, the type being designated as the ASaC7. The main role for the ASaC7 is the detection of low-flying attacking aircraft, interception/attack control and over-the-horizon targeting for ship-launched missiles. The radar is capable of simultaneously tracking up to 400 targets.

In 1982, during the Falklands War, Sea Kings of the RN proved to be remarkably versatile, being deployed mainly for ASW, but also for troop and supply transport, and supporting Special Air Service (SAS) forces. In 1991, during the first Gulf War, the Sea King was operated in a number of roles, including SAR and as a ship-to-ship logistics transport. During the blockade of Iraqi ports, Royal Marines (RM) were flown in Sea King helicopters to intercept any suspect ships that refused to stop or alter course.

Sea Kings operated by No.820 NAS and 845 NAS were deployed as part of the NATO intervention force in Bosnia.

Aircraft from 820 NAS were deployed from RFA ships to provided logistical support, ferrying troops and supplies across the Adriatic Sea. The squadron performed over 1,400 deck landings and flew in excess of 1,900 hours. The Sea Kings from No.845 NAS performed vital CASEVAC and other tasks, and many of these machines were damaged by hostile ground fire. Ship-based Sea Kings from No.814 NAS were deployed to the Kosovo region in the same conflict to provide SAR coverage, as well as troop and logistics transport. In 2003, during Operation Iraqi Freedom, Sea King helicopters were used to provide logistics support, and to transport Royal Marines into Kuwait from HMS *Ark Royal*, HMS *Ocean* and other ships operating offshore.

A total of 330 Westland Sea King helicopters were built, and the type was exported to Australia, Belgium, Egypt, Germany, India and Norway.

Westland Sea King HC.4

First flight: May 7, 1969
Power: 2 x Rolls-Royce Gnome H1400-1T turboshaft
Armament: None
Size: Rotor diameter – 18.9m/62ft
Length – 17.02m/55ft 10in
Height – 4.72m/15ft 6in
Weights: Empty – 5,620kg/12,390lb
Take-off – 9,752kg/21,500lb (maximum)
Performance: Speed – 245kph/152mph (maximum)
Service ceiling – 3,048m/10,000ft
Range – 1230km/764 miles

Westland Wasp and Scout

The Westland Wasp and Scout were small, gas turbine-powered, light military helicopters derived from the P.531 programme that began as a Saunders-Roe design before that company was absorbed by Westland. At one point, the naval aircraft was to be called Sea Scout. The Wasp differed from the land-based Scout by being fitted with a four-wheeled undercarriage (as opposed to a skid type) for easy manoeuvring on a flight deck. The Wasp also had increased fuel capacity for longer overwater operations, and a folding tail unit and rotor blades for easy stowage in the compact hangar on a frigate-sized ship.

The Wasp was a classic Cold War design that met a Royal Navy requirement for a small helicopter that could operate from the deck of a frigate and carry two homing torpedoes. This was to counter the improvement in speed and attack range of the Soviet submarine fleet, and to increase the range at which an enemy vessel could be detected and attacked. The Wasp was in effect a stand-off weapons system that gave the RN an anti-submarine reach beyond the range of any weapons carried on board on a warship of the time. However, the Wasp was not equipped with sonar or radar, and had to be guided to the target by radar operators on board the ship.

The prototype of the naval version was first flown on October 28, 1962, and production of 98 Wasp helicopters began almost immediately. From mid-1963, the type began to enter squadron service with the RN. As the more capable Westland Lynx entered service in the late 1970s, the Wasp was gradually withdrawn from

ABOVE: The Westland Scout AH Mk1 became operational with the British Army Air Corps (AAC) in 1963, and continued in service until 1994. For practicality, the machine was built with a skid-type undercarriage equipped with two small wheels as an aid to ground handling. The type was originally flown on observation and liason duties, but was later modified to carry four Nord SS.11 anti-tank missiles. The Scout was given the name "The Flying Jeep" by army aircrew, after the famous light utility vehicle of World War II.

ABOVE: The Westland Wasp was developed for the Royal Navy and fitted with a four-strut, double-wishbone undercarriage. The four wheels were self-castoring for operations on the landing deck of a warship. Later in Royal Navy service, the Wasp was modified to carry the Nord SS.11 wire-guided missile to target small surface vessels.

operational use. That was until 1982 and the Falklands War, when seven "mothballed" Type 22 frigates and their helicopters were recommissioned for active service in the South Atlantic. The Wasp was finally withdrawn from service in 1988, when the last of the frigates for which the helicopter had been designed was decommissioned.

From 1963, the Westland Scout AH Mk1 became an important element of the Army Air Corps (AAC) and, of the 150 ordered, 30 were still operational when the type was withdrawn from service in 1994. Known to aircrew as "The Flying Jeep", the Scout was used for observation, liaison and Casualty Evacuation (CASEVAC) duties. The type could also be configured as a light attack helicopter armed with two skid-mounted, forward-firing 7.62mm machine-gun packs or a single pintle-mounted machine-gun in the rear cabin. In the anti-tank role, the Scout was armed with four Nord SS.11 wire-guided missiles. In the CASEVAC role, the Scout could be fitted with two stretchers internally or two externally in pods mounted on the undercarriage.

RIGHT: **The Westland Scout was used operationally by the AAC in actions in various locations around the world. These included the Falklands campaign in 1982, where the type was used for many duties, such as supply, CASEVAC and ground attack.**

The type was used operationally in Aden, Borneo, Oman and Rhodesia. In Northern Ireland, AAC Scout helicopters were used for the rapid deployment of troops to set up surprise vehicle checkpoints to disrupt terrorist activity. The type could be fitted with a Nightsun high-power searchlight as an aid to night search operations..

The Scout was very much in the front line during the Falklands campaign. Twelve of the type were used to insert Special Air Service (SAS) personnel,

as well as supplying ammunition to front-line positions and recovering casualties for treatment. Two Scout helicopters were attacked by Argentine Air Force Pucara aircraft, and one was shot down – the only Argentine air-to-air victory of the war. The Scout was also used to attack enemy strongpoints. On June 14, an Argentine artillery position which was firing on advancing British troops was attacked and destroyed by Nord SS.11 anti-tank missiles fired from Scout helicopters at a range of 3,000m/3,281yd.

Few Scouts were exported, the only customers being Bahrain (2), Jordan (3) and Uganda (2). In 1963, two Westland Scout helicopters were acquired by the Royal Australian Navy (RAN), and were operated from survey ships until 1973.

BELOW: **The design for the type originated from the ex-Cierva team working at Saunders-Roe Limited.**

Westland Wasp HAS.1

First flight: October 28, 1962
Power: 1 x Rolls-Royce Nimbus Mk 503 turboshaft
Armament: Torpedoes, depth charges or anti-shipping missiles
Size: Rotor diameter – 9.83m/32ft 3in
Length – 9.24m/30ft 4in
Height – 3.56m/11ft 8in
Weights: Empty – 1,565kg/3,452lb (maximum)
Take-off – 2,495kg/5,500lb
Performance: Speed – 193kph/120mph (maximum)
Service ceiling – 3,813m/12,500ft
Range – 488km/303 miles

Westland Lynx

A British Army requirement for a multi-role helicopter to replace the Westland Scout was announced in 1964. The specification detailed a machine to carry seven fully armed troops, a 6,614kg/3,000lb load, and be operated in the CASEVAC, reconnaissance or liaison role. Westland Helicopters was contracted to design, build and develop the new machine that would enter service as the Lynx. Significantly, the new helicopter also had to be compact enough to be air-transportable in a Lockheed C-130 Hercules. In addition, Westland identified a Royal Navy requirement for a second-generation helicopter to operate from ships in adverse weather. In France, the military also had a requirement for an armed reconnaissance and ASW helicopter. The result was an Anglo–French agreement under which Westland would produce 70 per cent of each aircraft and Aérospatiale in France the balance. Significantly, the Lynx was the first British aircraft designed using metric rather than imperial measurements.

The prototype Lynx was first flown in 1971. The design utilized many components previously used in the Scout and Wasp helicopters. The rotor design was, however, all new and of honeycomb sandwich construction. In 1972, a Lynx was used to break the world helicopter speed record over distance for both 15 and 25km (9 and 15.5 miles) flown at 321.73kph/199.92mph. A short time later,

ABOVE: **The Westland Lynx has been in service with the Royal Navy since 1972, and has been used in combat during the Falklands campaign and both Gulf Wars in Iraq. For the anti-submarine warfare role, the Lynx is armed with the Mk 46 lightweight homing torpedo.**

the type was used to set a new 100km/62 miles closed circuit record, at a speed of 318.504kph/197.91mph.

ABOVE: **Westland proposed the Lynx 3 to the Army Air Corps as a purpose-built attack helicopter. The type was not ordered for production, and all development was cancelled.**

LEFT: **A Westland Lynx Mk3 was used as the development for the Lynx Mk8, which is currently in Royal Navy service. The type is equipped with the Sea Owl thermal imager in a turret mounting. The scanner for the Sea Spray radar is housed in a radome mounted under the nose of the aircraft.**

The first naval version, fitted with a lengthened nose to enclose a radar scanner, tricycle undercarriage and a deck restraint system, was flown in 1972. On June 29, 1973, the first landing trials at sea took place from the deck of RFA *Engadine*, a ship of the Royal Fleet Auxiliary (RFA).

An order for 113 of the Westland Lynx AH.1 (Army Helicopter Mark 1) was placed for service with the British Army to be used in the transport, anti-tank warfare (carrying eight TOW missiles) and reconnaissance roles. In 1977, deliveries of the first production Lynxes began to reach to the British Army. These machines were later upgraded to AH.7 standard with a strengthened airframe, an improved tail rotor, more sophisticated avionic and defensive equipment. Infra-red suppressors were fitted over the exhausts from each engine.

The first production Lynx HAS Mk2 was flown in 1976, and deck-handling trials at sea on HMS *Birmingham* (D86), a Type 42 destroyer, began in February 1977. In 1978, No. 702 Naval Air Squadron (NAS) based at RNAS Yeovilton, Somerset, was the first Royal Navy squadron to be equipped with the Lynx. The HAS Mk2 was developed principally for anti-submarine warfare and to be operated from the flight deck of destroyers and frigates. A total of 80 of the type were delivered to the RN, with the last 20 machines (designated HAS Mk3) being fitted with uprated

engines. The type was widely used by the French Navy as the Lynx Mk2 (FN) and Mk4 (FN) respectively.

Some 25 Lynx helicopters were deployed by the Royal Navy during the Falklands War. On April 25, 1982, the type was first used in an action in an attack on the *Santa Fe*, an Argentine Navy submarine. The Lynx was deployed during Operation Desert Storm (first Gulf War), and those in RN service were used to attack ships of the Iraqi Navy with the Sea Skua anti-shipping missile.

In 1986, a modified Lynx flown by Westland test pilot John Egginton set an absolute speed record for helicopters over 15 and 25km (9 and 15.5 miles) of 400.87kph/249.09mph. The Lynx remains one of the most agile military helicopters in the world and, being cleared for aerobatics, has equipped "The Black Cats", the Royal Navy helicopter display team formed by pilots of No.702 NAS.

The Lynx Mk7 currently in service with the Fleet Air Arm (FAA) is operated as an attack/utility helicopter in support of the Royal Marines. The Lynx HMA Mk8 is an ASW helicopter equipped with the Sea Skua anti-shipping missile operating from RN warships. During the invasion of Iraq in 2003, a Lynx from No.847 NAS was shot down over Basra, on May 6, 2006. The Lynx began being phased out of service with the Royal Navy from 2012.

In June 2006, the Ministry of Defence awarded AgustaWestland a contract to develop a "super" Lynx helicopter, incorporating advanced technology to provide an increased operational capability. The AW159 Lynx Wildcat has been designed to have a high level of commonality in airframe, avionics and cockpit equipment. More powerful engines are fitted to provide the type with an improvement in speed, endurance and economy. The most visible changes include a redesigned nose and rear fuselage, a tailplane with endplates and an improved tail rotor.

The Lynx has been operated by the navies of Argentina, Brazil, Denmark, Egypt, Germany, Portugal, Norway, the Netherlands, Nigeria and South Korea. The Army Air Corps (AAC) were the only operators of the battlefield version.

Westland Lynx HAS.8

First flight: March 21, 1971
Power: 2 x Rolls-Royce Gem 42-1 turboshaft
Armament: Torpedoes, depth charges, anti-shipping missile or anti-tank missile
Size: Rotor diameter – 12.8m/42ft
  Length – 15.24m/50ft
  Height – 3.76m/12ft 1in
Weights: Empty – 3,291kg/7,255lb
  Take-off – 5,125kg/11,300lb (maximum)
Performance: Speed – 232kph/144mph (maximum)
  Service ceiling – 2,576m/8,450ft
  Range – 275km/171 miles

Index

LEFT: **Bell UH-1 Iroquois.**